THE COLOR OF A GREAT CITY

The City of My Dreams

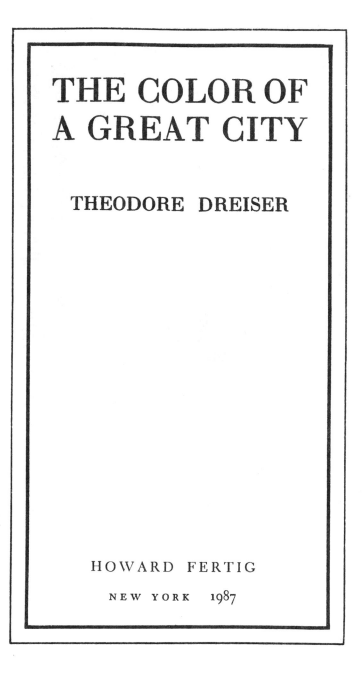

THE COLOR OF
A GREAT CITY

THEODORE DREISER

HOWARD FERTIG

NEW YORK 1987

Copyright 1923 by Boni and Liveright, Inc.
Renewal copyright © 1951 by Mrs. Theodore Dreiser
Howard Fertig, Inc. Edition 1987
Published by arrangement with the Dreiser Trust
All rights reserved.

Library of Congress Cataloging-in-Publication Data
Dreiser, Theodore, 1871–1945.
    The color of a great city.
    Reprint. Originally published: New York :
Boni and Liveright, 1923.
    1. New York (N.Y.)—Description.   2. New York
(N.Y.)—Social conditions.   I. Title.
F128.5.D77   1987   974.7'1041   86-27128
ISBN 0-86527-353-7

Printed in the United States of America

FOREWORD

My only excuse for offering these very brief pictures of the City of New York as it was between 1900 and 1914 or '15, or thereabout, is that they are of the very substance of the city I knew in my early adventurings in it. Also, and more particularly, they represent in part, at least, certain phases which at that time most arrested and appealed to me, and which now are fast vanishing or are no more. I refer more particularly to such studies as *The Bread-line, The Push-cart Man, The Toilers of the Tenements, Christmas in the Tenements, Whence the Song,* and *The Love Affairs of Little Italy.*

For, to begin with, the city, as I see it, was more varied and arresting and, after its fashion, poetic and even idealistic then than it is now. It offered, if I may venture the opinion, greater social and financial contrasts than it does now: the splendor of the purely social Fifth Avenue of the last decade of the last century and the first decade of this, for instance, as opposed to the purely commercial area that now bears that name; the sparklingly personality-dotted Wall Street of 1890-1910 as contrasted with the commonplace and almost bread and butter world that it is to-day. (There were argonauts then.) The astounding areas of poverty and of beggary even,– I refer to the east side and the Bowery of that period—unrelieved as they were by civic betterment and social service ventures of all kinds, as contrasted with the beschooled and beserviced east side of to-day. Who re-

calls Steve Brodies, McGurks, Doyers Street and
"Chuck" Connors?

The city is larger. It has, if you will, more amazing
architectural features. But has it as vivid and moving
social contrasts,—as hectic and poignant and disturbing
mental and social aspirations as it had then? I cannot
see that it has. Rather, as it seems to me, it is duller because less differentiated. There are millions and millions but what do they do? Tramp aimlessly, for the
most part, here and there in shoals, to see a ball game,
a football game, a parade, a prize-fight, a civic betterment or automobile exhibition or to dance or dine in a
hall that holds a thousand. But of that old zest that
seemed to find something secret and thrilling in a thousand nooks and corners of the old city, its Bowery, its
waterfront, its rialto, its outlying resorts, not a trace.
One cannot even persuade the younger generation, that
never even knew the old city, to admit that they feel a
tang of living equivalent to what they imagined once
was. The truth is that it is not here. It has vanished
—along with the generation that felt it.

The pictures that I offer here, however, are not, I am
compelled to admit, of that more distinguished and
vibrant crust, which my introduction so far would imply.
Indeed they are the very antithesis, I think, of all that
glitter and glister that made the social life of that day
so superior. Its shadow, if you will, its reverse face.
For being very much alone at the time, and having of
necessity, as the situation stood, ample hours in which
to wander here and there, without, however, sufficient
financial means to divert myself in any other way, I was
given for the most part to rambling in what to me were

the strangest and most peculiar and most interesting areas I could find as contrasted with those of great wealth and to speculating at length upon the phases and the forces of life I then found so lavishly spread before me. The splendor of the, to me, new dynamic, new-world metropolis! Its romance, its enthusiasm, its illusions, its difficulties! The immense crowds everywhere —upon Manhattan Island, at least. The beautiful rivers and the bay with its world of shipping that washed its shores. Indeed, I was never weary of walking and contemplating the great streets, not only Fifth Avenue and Broadway, but the meaner ones also, such as the Bowery, Third Avenue, Second Avenue, Elizabeth Street in the lower Italian section and East Broadway. And at that time even (1894) that very different and most radically foreign plexus, known as the East Side, already stretched from Chatham Square and even farther south—Brooklyn Bridge—north to Fourteenth Street. For want of bridges and subways the city was not, as yet, so far-flung but for that reason more concentrated and almost as congested.

Yet before I was fifteen years in the city, all of the additional bridges, other than Brooklyn Bridge which was here when I came and which so completely served to change New York from the thing it was then to what it is now, were already in place—Manhattan, Williamsburg, Queens Borough Bridges. And the subways had been built, at least in part. But before then, if anything, the great island, as I have said, was even more compact of varied and foreign groups, and one had only to wander casually and not at any great length to come upon the Irish in the lower East and West Sides; the Syrians

in Washington Street—a great mass of them; the Greeks
around 26th, 27th and 28th Streets on the West Side; the
Italians around Mulberry Bend; the Bohemians in East
67th Street, and the Sicilians in East 116th Street and
thereabouts. The Jews were still chiefly on the East Side.

Being fascinated by these varying nationalities, and
their neighborhoods, I was given for the first year or two
of my stay here to wandering among them, as well as
along and through the various parks, the waterfronts
and the Bowery, and thinking, thinking, thinking on this
welter of life and the difficulties and the strangeness of
it. The veritable tides of people that were forever moving here—so different to the Middle-West cities I had
known. And the odd, or at least different, devices and
trades by which they made their way—the small shops,
trades, tricks even. For one thing, I was often given to
wondering how so many people could manage to subsist
in New York by grinding hand organs alone, or shining
shoes or selling newspapers or peanuts, or fruits or vegetables from a small stand or cart.

And the veritable shoals and worlds, even, of beggars
and bums and idlers and crooks in the Bowery and elsewhere. Indeed I was more or less dumbfounded by the
numerical force of these and the far cry it was from
them to the mansions in Fifth Avenue, the great shops
in Sixth Avenue and Twenty-third Street, the world
famous banking houses and personalities in Wall Street,
the comfortable cliff-dwellers who occupied the hotels and
apartment houses of the upper West Side and along
Broadway. For being young and inexperienced and
penniless, these economic differences had more significance for me then than they have since been able to

maintain. Yet always and primarily fascinated by the
problem of life itself, the riddle of its origin, the difficulties seemingly attending its maintenance everywhere,
such a polyglot city as this was, was not only an economic problem, but a strange and mysterious picture,
and I was never weary of spying out how the other fellow
lived and how he made his way. And yet how many
years it was, really, after I arrived here, quite all of
ten, before it ever occurred to me that apart from the
novel or short story, these particular scenes and my own
cogitations in connection might possess merit as pictures.

And so it was that not before 1904—ten years later,
really—that I was so much as troubled to sketch a single
impression of all that I had seen and then only at the
request of a Sunday editor of a New York newspaper
who was short of "small local stuff" to fill in between
his more lurid features. And even at that, not more
than seven or eight of all that are here assembled were at
that time even roughly sketched,—*The Bowery Mission,
The Waterfront, The Cradle of Tears, The Track Walker,
The Realization of an Ideal, The Log of a Harbor Pilot.*
Later, however, in 1908 and '09, finding space in a magazine of my own—*The Bohemian*—as well as one conducted by Senator Watson of Georgia, and bethinking
me of all I had seen and how truly wonderful and colorful it really was, I began to try to do more of them, and
at that time wrote at least seven or eight more—*The
Flight of Pigeons, Six O'clock, The Wonder of Water,
The Men in the Storm,* and *The Men in the Dark.* The
exact titles of all, apart from these, I have forgotten.

Still later, after the opening of the World War, and
because I was noting how swiftly and steadily the city
was changing and old landmarks and conditions were
being done away with, I thought it worth while to bring

together, not only all the scenes I had previously published or sketched, but to add some others which from
time to time I had begun but never finished.   Among
these at that time were *The Fire, Hell's Kitchen, A Wayplace of the Fallen, The Man on the Bench.*   And then,
several years ago, having in the meanwhile once more
laid aside the material to the advantage of other
matters, I decided that it was still worth while.   And
getting them all out and casting aside those I no longer
cared for, and rewriting others of which I approved,
together with new pictures of old things I had seen,
i.e., *Bums, The Michael J. Powers Association, A Vanished Summer Resort, The Push-cart Man, The Sandwich Man, Characters, The Men in the Snow, The City
Awakes*—I finally evolved the present volume.   But
throughout all these latest additions I sought only to
recapture the flavor and the color of that older day—
nothing more.   If they are anything, they are mere rep-
resentations of the moods that governed me at the time
that I had observed this material at first hand—not as I
know the city to be now.

In certain of these pictures, as will be seen, reference
is made to wages, hours and working and living conditions not now holding, or at least not to the same
severe degree.   This is especially true of such presenta-
tions as *The Men in the Dark, The Men in the Storm,
The Men in the Snow, Six O'clock, The Bread-line,*
(long since abolished), *The Toilers of the Tenements,*
and *Christmas in the Tenements.*   Yet since they were
decidedly true of that particular period, I prefer to
leave them as originally written.   They bear, I believe,
the stamp of their hour.

THEODORE DREISER.

CONTENTS

CONTENTS

THE COLOR OF A GREAT CITY

THE CITY OF MY DREAMS

It was silent, the city of my dreams, marble and serene, due perhaps to the fact that in reality I knew nothing of crowds, poverty, the winds and storms of the inadequate that blow like dust along the paths of life. It was an amazing city, so far-flung, so beautiful, so dead. There were tracks of iron stalking through the air, and streets that were as cañons, and stairways that mounted in vast flights to noble plazas, and steps that led down into deep places where were, strangely enough, underworld silences. And there were parks and flowers and rivers. And then, after twenty years, here it stood, as amazing almost as my dream, save that in the waking the flush of life was over it. It possessed the tang of contests and dreams and enthusiasms and delights and terrors and despairs. Through its ways and cañons and open spaces and underground passages were running, seething, sparkling, darkling, a mass of beings such as my dream-city never knew.

The thing that interested me then as now about New York—as indeed about any great city, but more definitely New York because it was and is so preponderantly large —was the sharp, and at the same time immense, contrast it showed between the dull and the shrewd, the strong

1

and the weak, the rich and the poor, the wise and the ignorant. This, perhaps, was more by reason of numbers and opportunity than anything else, for of course humanity is much the same everywhere. But the number from which to choose was so great here that the strong, or those who ultimately dominated, were so very strong, and the weak so very, very weak—and so very, very many.

I once knew a poor, half-demented, and very much shriveled little seamstress who occupied a tiny hall-bedroom in a side-street rooming-house, cooked her meals on a small alcohol stove set on a bureau, and who had about space enough outside of this to take three good steps either way.

"I would rather live in my hall-bedroom in New York than in any fifteen-room house in the country that I ever saw," she commented once, and her poor little colorless eyes held more of sparkle and snap in them than I ever saw there, before or after. She was wont to add to her sewing income by reading fortunes in cards and tea-leaves and coffee-grounds, telling of love and prosperity to scores as lowly as herself, who would never see either. The color and noise and splendor of the city as a spectacle was sufficient to pay her for all her ills.

And have I not felt the glamour of it myself? And do I not still? Broadway, at Forty-second Street, on those selfsame spring evenings when the city is crowded with an idle, sightseeing cloud of Westerners; when the doors of all shops are open, the windows of nearly all restaurants wide to the gaze of the idlest passer-by. Here

is the great city, and it is lush and dreamy. A May
or June moon will be hanging like a burnished silver
disc between the high walls aloft. A hundred, a thousand electric signs will blink and wink. And the floods
of citizens and visitors in summer clothes and with gay
hats; the street cars jouncing their endless carloads on
indifferent errands; the taxis and private cars fluttering about like jeweled flies. The very gasoline con-
tributes a distinct perfume. Life bubbles, sparkles;
chatters gay, incoherent stuff. Such is Broadway.

And then Fifth Avenue, that singing, crystal street,
on a shopping afternoon, winter, summer, spring or
fall. What tells you as sharply of spring when, its windows crowded with delicate effronteries of silks and gay
nothings of all description, it greets you in January,
February and March? And how as early as November
again, it sings of Palm Beach and Newport and the lesser
or greater joys of the tropics and the warmer seas. And
in September, how the haughty display of furs and rugs,
in this same avenue, and costumes de luxe for ball and
dinner, cry out of snows and blizzards, when you are
scarcely ten days back from mountain or seaside. One
might think, from the picture presented and the residences which line the upper section, that all the world
was inordinately prosperous and exclusive and happy.
And yet, if you but knew the tawdry underbrush of
society, the tangle and mat of futile growth between the
tall trees of success, the shabby chambers crowded with
aspirants and climbers, the immense mansions barren
of a single social affair, perfect and silent!

I often think of the vast mass of underlings, boys and

girls, who, with nothing but their youth and their ambitions to commend them, are daily and hourly setting their faces New Yorkward, reconnoitering the city for what it may hold in the shape of wealth or fame, or, if not that, position and comfort in the future; and what, if anything, they will reap. Ah, their young eyes drinking in its promise! And then, again, I think of all the powerful or semi-powerful men and women throughout the world, toiling at one task or another—a store, a mine, a bank, a profession—somewhere outside of New York, whose one ambition is to reach the place where their wealth will permit them to enter and remain in New York, dominant above the mass, luxuriating in what they consider luxury.

The illusion of it, the hypnosis deep and moving that it is! How the strong and the weak, the wise and the fools, the greedy of heart and of eye, seek the nepenthe, the Lethe, of its something hugeness. I always marvel at those who are willing, seemingly, to pay any price— *the* price, whatever it may be—for one sip of this poison cup. What a stinging, quivering zest they display. How beauty is willing to sell its bloom, virtue its last rag, strength an almost usurious portion of that which it controls, youth its very best years, its hope or dream of fame, fame and power their dignity and presence, age its weary hours, to secure but a minor part of all this, a taste of its vibrating presence and the picture that it makes. Can you not hear them almost, singing its praises?

THE CITY AWAKES

HAVE you ever arisen at dawn or earlier in New York and watched the outpouring in the meaner side-streets or avenues? It is a wondrous thing. It seems to have so little to do with the later, showier, brisker life of the day, and yet it has so very much. It is in the main so drab or shabby-smart at best, poor copies of what you see done more efficiently later in the day. Typewriter girls in almost stage or society costumes entering shabby offices; boys and men made up to look like actors and millionaires turning into the humblest institutions, where they are clerks or managers. These might be called the machinery of the city, after the elevators and street cars and wagons are excluded, the implements by which things are made to go.

Take your place on Williamsburg Bridge some morning, for instance, at say three or four o'clock, and watch the long, the quite unbroken line of Jews trundling pushcarts eastward to the great Wallabout Market over the bridge. A procession out of Assyria or Egypt or Chaldea, you might suppose, Biblical in quality; or, better yet, a huge chorus in some operatic dawn scene laid in Paris or Petrograd or here. A vast, silent mass it is, marching to the music of necessity. They are so grimy, so mechanistic, so elemental in their movements and needs. And later on you will find them seated or standing, with their little charcoal buckets or braziers to warm their hands and feet, in those gusty, icy streets of the East Side in winter, or coatless and almost shirtless in hot weather, open-mouthed for want of air. And they are New York, too —Bucharest and Lemberg and Odessa come to the Bowery, and adding rich, dark, colorful threads to the rug or tapestry which is New York.

Since these are but a portion, think of those other masses that come from the surrounding territory, north, south, east and west. The ferries—have you ever observed them in the morning? Or the bridges, railway terminals, and every elevated and subway exit?

Already at six and six-thirty in the morning they have begun to trickle small streams of human beings Manhattan or cityward, and by seven and seven-fifteen these streams have become sizable affairs. By seven-thirty and eight they have changed into heavy, turbulent rivers, and by eight-fifteen and eight-thirty and nine they are raging torrents, no less. They overflow all the streets and avenues and every available means of conveyance. They are pouring into all available doorways, shops, factories, office-buildings—those huge affairs towering so significantly above them. Here they stay all day long, causing those great hives and their adjacent streets to flush with a softness of color not indigenous to them, and then at night, between five and six, they are going again, pouring forth over the bridges and through the subways and across the ferries and out on the trains, until the last drop of them appears

to have been exuded, and they are pocketed in some
outlying side-street or village or metropolitan hall-room
—and the great, turbulent night of the city is on once
more. And yet they continue to stream cityward,—this cityward. From all parts of the world they are pouring
into New York: Greeks from Athens and the realms of
Sparta and Macedonia, living six, seven, eight, nine, ten,
eleven, twelve, in one room, sleeping on the floors and
dressing and eating and entertaining themselves God
knows how; Jews from Russia, Poland, Hungary, the
Balkans, crowding the East Side and the inlying sections
of Brooklyn, and huddling together in thick, gummy
streets, singing in street crowds around ballad-mongers
of the woes of their native land, seeking with a kind
of divine, poetic flare a modicum of that material comfort which their natures so greatly crave, which their
previous condition for at least fifteen hundred years
has scarcely warranted; Italians from Sicily and the
warmer vales of the South, crowding into great sections
of their own, all hungry for a taste of New York; Germans, Hungarians, French, Polish, Swedish, Armenians,
all with sections of their own and all alive to the joys
of the city, and how eager to live—great gold and scarlet
streets throbbing with the thoughts of them!

And last but not least, the illusioned American from
the Middle West and the South and the Northwest and
the Far West, crowding in and eyeing it all so eagerly,
so yearningly, like the others. Ah, the little, shabby,
blue-light restaurants! The boarding houses in silent

streets! The moral, hungry "homes"—how full they are of them and how hopeless! How the city sings and sings for them, and in spite of them, flaunting ever afresh its lures and beauties—a city as wonderful and fateful and ironic as life itself.

THE WATERFRONT

WERE I asked to choose a subject which would most gratify my own fancy I believe I would choose the docks and piers of New York. Nowhere may you find a more pleasingly encouraging picture-life going on at a leisurely gait, but going, nor one withal set in a lovelier framework. And, personally, I have always foolishly imagined that the laborers and men of affairs connected with them must be the happier for that connection. It is more than probable that that is not true, but what can be more interesting than long, heavily-laden piers jutting out into the ever-flowing waters of a river? And those tall masts adjoining, how they rock and swing! Whistler had a fancy for scenes like these; they appealed to his sense of line and background and romance. You can look at his etchings of collections of boats along the Thames at London and see how keenly he must have felt the beauty of what he saw. Networks of ropes and spars; stout, stodgy figures of half-idle laborers; delicious, comforting, homey suggestions of houses and spires behind; and then the water.

How the water sips and gurgles about these stanchions and spiles and hulls! You stand on the shore or on the hard-cobbled streets of the waterfront, crowded with trucks and cars, and you realize that the too, too solid substance of which they are composed is to be here for years. But this water at your feet, this dark, silent current sipping about the boats and rocking them, the big boats and the little boats, is running away. Here comes a chip, there goes a wisp of straw. A tomato box comes leisurely bobbing upon the surface of the stream, and now a tug heaves into view, puffing and blowing, and then a great "liner" being towed to her dock. And then these nearer boats fastened here— how they rest and swing in the summer sunshine! No rush, no hurry. Only slow movement. Yet all are surely and gradually slipping away. In an hour your ship will be a mile or two farther down stream. In a day or two or three your liner will be once more upon the bosom of the broad Atlantic or, later even, the Pacific. The tug you saw towing it will be pulling at something else, or you will find it shoving its queer stubby nose into some quaint angle of the waterside, hardly earning its skipper's salt. Is it not a delicious, lovely, romantic picture? And yet with the tang of change and decay in it too, the gradual passing of all things—yourself—myself—all.

As for the vast piers on the shores of the Hudson, the East River, the Jersey side and Brooklyn and Staten Island, where the liners house themselves, I cannot fancy anything more colorful. They come from all ports of the world, these big ships. They bring tremendous cargoes, not only of people but of goods, and they carry large forces of men, to say nothing of those who assist them to load and unload. If you watch any of the waterfronts to and from which they make their entry and departure you will find that you can easily tell when they are

loading and unloading. The broad, expansive street-
fronts before these piers are crowded with idling men
waiting for the opportunity to work, the call of duty
or of necessity. And it is an interesting crowd of men
always, this, imposingly large on occasion. Individually
these men are crude but appealing, the kind of man that
is usually and truly dubbed a workingman. They have
in the main, rough, quaint, ambling figures, and rougher,
ruder hands and faces. Some of them are black from
having shoveled in the holds of vessels or passed coal
(coal-passers is their official title), and some are dusky
and strawy from having juggled boxes and bales, but
they are men who with a small capacity for mental
analysis are taking things exactly as they find them.
They are not even possessed of a trade, unless you would
call the art of piling boxes and bales under the direction
of a foreman a trade. Apparently they have no sense of
the sociologic or economic arrangement of life, no com-
prehension of the position which they occupy in the
affairs of the world. They know they are laborers and as
such subject to every whim and fancy of their masters.
They stand or sit like sheep in droves awaiting the call
of opportunity. You see them in sun or rain, on hot days
and cold ones, waiting here. Sometimes they jest, sometimes they talk, sometimes they sit and wait. But the
water with which they are so intimately connected, from
which they draw their subsistence, flows on. I have seen
a vain, self-conscious foreman come out from one of these
great pier buildings and with a Cæsar-like wave of his
hand beckon to this man and that. At his sign a dozen,
a score of men would rise and look inquiringly in his

direction, dumb and patient like cattle. And then he would pick this one and that, wavering subtly over his choice, pushing aside this one, who was not quite strong enough, perhaps, or agile enough, laying a hand favoringly on that, and then turning eventually and leaving the remaining members of the group dumb but a little disappointed. Invariably they seemed to me to be a bit bereaved and neglected, sorry that they could not help themselves, but still willing to wait. I have sometimes thought that cattle are better provided for, or at least as well.

But from an artistic and natural point of view the scene has always fascinated me. Is it morning? The sun sparkles on the waters, the wind blows free, gulls wheel and turn and squeal, white flecks above the water, swarms of vehicles gather with their loads, life seems to move at a smart clip. Is it noon? A large group of men is to be seen idling in the sun, blue-jacketed, swarthy-faced, colorful against the dark background of the piers. Is it night? The lanterns swing and rock. There is darkness overhead and the stars.

I sometimes think no human being ever lived who caught more significantly, more sweetly, the beauty of the waterfront than the great Englishman, Turner. When one looks at his canvases, rich in their gold of sunshine, their blue of sky, their haze of moisture, one feels all that the sea really presents. This man understood, as did Whistler, only he translated his mood in regard to it all into richer colors, those gorgeous golds, reds, pinks, greens, blues. And he had a greater tenderness for atmosphere than did Whistler. In Whistler one misses more than the bare facts, albeit deliciously, artistically, perfectly presented. In Turner one finds the facts presented as by nature in her balmiest mood, and idealized by the love and affection of the artist. You have seen "The Fighting Téméraire," of course. It is here in New York harbor any sunny afternoon. The wind dies down, the sun pours in a golden flood upon the east bank from the west, the tall elevator stacks and towering chimneys of factories on the west shore give a beauty of line which no artist could resist. Up the splashing bosom of the river, trembling silver and gold in the evening light, comes a great vessel. Her sides stand out blackly. Her masts and funnels, tinged with an evening glow of gold, burn and shimmer. Against a magnificent, a radiant sky, where red and gold clouds hang in broken patches, she floats, exquisitely penciled and colored— "The Fighting Téméraire." You would know her. Only it is now the Hudson and not the Thames.

The skyline, the ship masts, the sun, the water, all these are alike. The very ship is the same, apparently, and the sun drops down as it did that other day when his picture was painted. The stars come out, the masts rock, swinging their little lamps, the water runs sipping and sucking at the docks and piers. The winds blow cool, and there is silence until the morning. Then the waterfront assumes its quaint, delicious, easy atmosphere once more. It is once more fresh and free. So runs its tide, so runs its life, so runs our very world away.

THE LOG OF A HARBOR PILOT

An ocean pilot-boat lay off Tompkinsville of an early spring afternoon, in the stillest water. The sun was bright, and only the lightest wind was stirring. When we reached the end of the old cotton dock, an illustrator and myself, commissioned by a then but now no more popular magazine, there she was, a small, two-masted schooner of about fifty tons burden, rocking gently upon the water. We accepted the services of a hawking urchin, who had a canoe to rent, and who had followed us down the main street in the hope of earning a half-dollar. He led the way through a hole in a fence that enclosed the street at the water end and down a long, stilted plank walk to a mess of craft and rigging, where we found his little tub, and pushed out. In a few minutes we had crossed the quiet stretch of water and were alongside.

Like all pilot-boats, the *Hermann Oelrichs* was built low in the water, so that it was easy to jump aboard.

14

Her sails were furled and, from the quiet prevailing, one might have supposed that the crew had gone into the village. No sound issued until we reached the companionway. Then below we could see the cook scraping cold ashes out of a fireless stove. He was cleaning the cabin and putting things to rights before the pilots arrived. He accepted our intrusion with a friendly glance.

"Captain Rierson told us to come aboard," we said.

"All right, sir. Stow your things in any one of them bunks."

We went about this while the ashes were taken out and tossed overboard. When the cook returned it was with a bucket and brush, and he attacked the oilcloth on the floor industriously.

"Cozy little cabin, this, eh?"

"Yes, she's a comfortable little boat," replied the cook. "These pilots take things purty comfortable. She's not as fast as some of the boats, but she's all right in rough weather."

"Do you encounter much rough weather?"

"Well, now and again," answered the cook, with the vaguest suggestion of a twinkle in his eye. "It's purty rough sometimes in winter."

"How long do you stay out?"

"Sometimes three, sometimes five days, sometimes we get rid of all seven pilots the first day—there's no telling. It's all 'cording to how the steamers come in."

"So we may be out a week?"

"About that. Maybe ten days."

We went on deck. It was warm and bright. Some

sailors from the fore-hatch were scrubbing down the deck, which dried white and warm as fast as they swabbed off the water. Wide-winged gulls were circling high and low among the ships of the harbor. On Staten Island many a little curl of smoke rose from the chimneys of white cottages.

That evening the crew of five men kept quietly to their quarters and slept. The moon shone clear until ten, when the barometer suddenly fell and clouds came out of the east. By cock-crow it was raining, and by morning it was drizzling and cold.

The pilots appeared one after another. They came out to the edge of the cotton wharf through the mist and rain, and waved a handkerchief as a signal that a boat should be sent ashore for them. One or two, failing to attract the immediate attention of the crew, resorted to the expedient of calling out: "Schooner, Ahoy!" in voices which partook of some of the stoutness of the sea.

"Come ashore, will you?" they shouted, when a head appeared above deck.

No sooner were they recognized than the yawl was launched and sent ashore. They came aboard and descended quickly out of the rain into the only room (or cabin) at the foot of the companionway. This was at once their sitting-room, dining-room, bedroom, and every other chamber for the voyage. Here they stowed their satchels and papers in lockers beneath their individual sleeping berths. Each one sought out a stout canvas clothes bag, which all pilots use in lieu of a trunk, and began to unpack his ship's clothes. All took off their land apparel and dressed themselves in ancient

seat-patched and knee-worn garments, which were far
more comfortable than graceful, and every one produced the sailor's essential, a pipe and tobacco.

Dreary as was the day overhead, the atmosphere of
the cabin changed with their arrival. Not only was it
soon thick with the fumes of many pipes, but it was
bright with genial temper. Not one of the company of
seven pilots seemed moody.

"Whose watch is it?" asked one.

"Rierson's, I think," was the answer.

"He ain't here yet."

"Here he comes now."

At this a hale Norwegian, clean and hard as a pine
knot, came down the companionway.

"My turn to-day, eh? Are we all here?"

"Ay!" cried one.

"Then we might as well go, hey?"

"Ay! Ay! came the chorus.

"Steward!" he called. "Tell the men to hoist sail!"

"Ay! Ay! sir!" answered the steward.

Then were rattlings and clatterings overhead. While
the little company in the cabin were chatting, the work
on deck was resulting in a gradual change, and when,
after a half-hour, Rierson put his head out into
the wind and rain above the companionway, the cotton
docks were far in the rear, all but lost in the mist and
drizzle. All sails were up and a stiff breeze was driving
the little craft through the Narrows. McLaughlin, the
boatman and master of the crew, under Rierson, was
at the wheel. Already we were being rocked and tossed
like a child in a cradle.

"Who controls the vessel," I asked of him, "while the pilots are on board?"

"The pilots themselves."

"Not all of them?"

"No, not all at one time. The pilot who has the watch has full control for his hours, then the next pilot after him, and so on. No pilot is interfered with during his service."

"And where do we head now?"

"For Sandy Hook and the sea east of that. We are going to meet inbound European steamers."

The man at the wheel, McLaughlin, was a clean athletic young chap, with a straight, full nose and a clear, steady eye. In his yellow raincoat, rubber boots and "sou'-wester" he looked to be your true sea-faring man. With the little craft plunging ahead in a storm of wind and rain and over ever-increasing billows, he gazed out steadily and whistled an airy tune.

"You seem to like it," I remarked.

"Yes," he answered. "It's not a bad life. Rather cold in winter, but summer makes up for it. Then we're in port every fifth or sixth day on an average. Sometimes we get a night off."

"The pilots have it better than that?"

"Oh, yes; they get back quicker. The man who has the first watch may get back to-day, if we meet a steamer. They might all get back if we meet enough steamers."

"You put a man aboard each one?"

"Yes."

"How do you know when a steamer wants a pilot?"

"Well, we are in the track of incoming steamers. There is no other pilot-boat sailing back and forth on this partciular track at this time. If a steamer comes along she may show a signal for a pilot or she may turn a little in our direction. Either way, we know she wants one. Then we lay to and wait until she comes up. You'll see, though. One is likely to come along at any time now.''

The interior of the little craft presented a peculiar contrast to storm and sea without. In the fore compartment stood the cook at his stove preparing the midday meal. Sailors, when no orders were called from above, lay in their bunks, which curved toward the prow. The pots and pans of the stove moved restlessly about with the swell. The cook whistled, timbers creaked, the salt spray swished above the hatch, and mingled odors of meats and vegetables combined and thickened the air.

In the after half of the boat were the pilots, making the best of idle time. No steamer was sighted, and so they lounged and smoked. Two or three told of difficulties on past voyages. Two of the stoutest and jolliest were met in permanent conflict over a game of pinochle. One read, the others took down pillows from the bunks, and spreading them out on the wide seat that lined two sides of the room, snored profoundly. Nearly all took turns, before or after games, or naps, at smoking. Sometimes all smoked. It was observable that no "listener" was necessary for conversation. Some talked loudly, without a single person heeding. At times all talked at once in those large imperious voices which seem common to the sea. The two old pilots at cards never halted. Storms might come and storms might go; they paused only to renew their pipes.

At the wheel, in tarpaulin and sou'wester, McLaughlin kept watch. Sea spray kept his cheeks dripping. His coat was glassy with water. Another pilot put his head above deck.

"How are we heading?"

"East by no'."

"See anything?"

"A steamer, outbound."

"Which one?"

"The *Tauric.*"

"Wish she was coming in!" concluded the inquirer, as he went below.

We kept before the wind in this driving way. All the morning and all the afternon the rain fell. The cook served a wholesome meal of meats and vegetables, and afterwards all pipes were set smoking more industriously than ever. The two old pilots renewed their cards. Every one turned to trifling diversions, with the feeling that he must get comfort out of them. It was a little drowsy, a little uncomfortable, a little apt to make one long for shore. In the midst of the lull the voice of the man at the wheel sounded at the companionway.

"Steamer on the port bow! Pilot-boat Number Nine! She's hailing us."

"Well, what does she want?"

"Can't make out yet."

One and all hastened on deck. On our left, in the

fog and rain, tossed a little steamer which was recognized as the steam pilot-boat stationed at Sandy Hook. She was starboarding to come nearer and several of her pilots and crew were at her rail hailing us. As she approached, keener ears made out that she wanted to put two men aboard us.

"We don't want any more men aboard here," said one. "We've got seven now."

"No!" said several in chorus. "Tell 'em we can't take 'em."

"We can't take any more," shouted the helmsman, in long-drawn sounds. "We've got seven aboard now."

"Orders to put two men aboard ye," came back over the tumbling waters. "We've a sick man."

"Don't let 'em put any more men aboard here. Where they goin' to sleep?" argued another. "One man's got to bunk it as it is, unless we lose one pretty soon."

"How you goin' to help it? They're puttin' their men out."

"Head away! Head away! They can't come aboard if you head away!"

"Oh, well; it's too late now."

It was really too late, for the steamer had already cast a yawl and the two men, together with the crew, were in it and heading over the churning water. All watched them as they came alongside and clambered on.

They were Jersey pilots who had been displaced on the other boat because one of their number had been taken sick and more room was needed to make him comfortable. He was thought to be dying, and must be taken back to New York at once, and his condition formed the topic of conversation for the rest of the day.

Meanwhile our schooner headed outward, with nothing to reward her search. At five o'clock there was some talk of not finding anything before mórning. Several advised running toward Princess Bay on Staten Island and into stiller water, and as the minutes passed the feeling crystallized. In a few minutes all were urging a tack toward port, and soon it was done. Sails were shifted, the prow headed shoreward, and gradually, as the track of the great vessels was abandoned, the waters became less and less rough, then more and more quiet, until finally, when we came within distant sight of Princess Bay and the Staten Island shore, the little vessel only rocked from side to side; the pitching and churning were over.

It was windy and cold on deck, however, and after the crew had dropped anchor they remained below. There was nothing to do save idle the time. The few oil lamps, the stove-fire and the clearing away of dishes after supper, gave the cabin of the fore-and-aft a very home-like appearance.

Forward, most of the sailors stretched in their bunks to digest their meal. There were a few magazines and papers on the table, a few decks of cards and a set of checkers. It was interesting to note the genial mood of the men. One might fancy oneself anywhere but at sea, save for the rocking of the boat. It was more like a farmhouse kitchen. One little old sailor, grizzled and lean, had only recently escaped from a Hongkong trader, where he had been sadly abused. Another was a mere boy, who belonged to Staten Island. He had been working in a canning factory all winter, he said, but had decided to go to sea for a change. It was not his first experience; this alternating was a regular thing with him. The summer previous he had worked as cook's scullion on one of the other pilot-boats; this summer he was a sailor.

The Staten Islander had the watch on deck from ten to twelve that night. By that time the rain had ceased and the lights on the distant shore were visible, glimmering faintly, it seemed good to be on deck. The wind blew slightly chill and the waters sipped and sucked at the prow and sides. Coming above I chatted with the young sailor.

"Do you like sea life?" I asked him.

"There ain't much to it."

"Would you rather be on shore?"

"Well, if I didn't have to work so hard."

"You like one, then, as well as the other?"

"Well, on shore the hours are longer, but you get your evenings and Sundays. Out here there ain't any hour your own, but there's plenty days when there's nothin' doin'. Some days there ain't no wind. Sometimes we cruise right ahead without touchin' the sails. Still, it's hard, 'cause you can't see nobody."

"What would you do if you were on shore?"

"Oh, go to the show."

It developed that his heart yearned for "nights off." The little, bright-windowed main street in New Brighton was to his vision a kind of earthly heaven. To be there of an evening when people were passing, to loaf on the corner and see the bright-eyed girls go by, to be in the village hubbub, was to him the epitome of living. The great, silent, suggestive sea meant nothing to him.

After a while he went below and tumbled in and McLaughlin, the boatman, took the turn. In the cabin most of the pilots had gone to bed. Yet the two old salts were still at pinochle, browbeating each other, but in a subdued tone. All pipes were out. Snores were numerous and long.

At dawn the pilot whose turn it was to guide the next steamer into New York took the wheel. We sailed out into the east and the morning, looking for prey. It came soon, in the shape of a steamer.

"Steamer!" called the pilot, and all the other pilots turned out and came on deck. The sea to the eastward, whither they were looking, was utterly bare of craft. Not a sail, not a wisp of smoke! Yet they saw something and tacked ship so as to swing round and sail toward it. Not even the telescope revealed it to my untrained eyes until five minutes had gone by, when afar off a speck appeared above the waters. It came on larger and larger, until it assumed the proportions of a toy.

With the first announcement of a steamer the pilot who was to take this one in gave the wheel to the pilot who was to have the next one. He seemed pleased at getting back to New York so soon. While the ship was coming forward he went below and changed his clothes. In a few minutes he was on deck, dressed in a neat business suit and white linen. His old clothes had all been packed in a grain sack. He had a bundle of New York papers and a light overcoat over his arm.

"How did you know that steamer wanted a pilot?"
I asked him.

"I could tell by the way she was heading."

"Do you think she saw you?"

"Yes."

"Can you always tell when a steamer so far off wants a pilot?"

"Nearly always. If we can't judge by her course we can see through the telescope whether she has a signal for a pilot flying."

"And when you go aboard her what will you do?"

"Go to the bridge and direct her course."

"Do you take the wheel or do any work?"

"Not at all."

"What about your breakfast?"

"I'll take that with the officers of the deck."

"Do you always carry a bundle of papers?"

"Sure. The officers and passengers like to get early news of New York. Sometimes the papers are pretty old before we hand them out, but they're better than nothing."

He studied the approaching steamer closely through the glass.

"The *Ems*," he said laconically. "Get the yawl ready, boys."

Four sailors went to the lee side and righted the boat there. The great vessel was plowing toward us at a fine rate. Every minute she grew larger, until at half a mile she seemed quite natural.

"Heave the yawl," called the man at the wheel.

Over went the boat with a splash, and two men after

and into it. They held it close to the side of the schooner until the departing pilot could jump in.

"Cast loose!" said the man at the wheel to the men holding the rope.

"Ay! Ay! sir!" they replied.

"Good-by, Billie," called the pilots.

"So long, boys," he cried back.

Our schooner was moving swiftly away before the wind. The man in the yawl pulled out toward where the steamer must pass. Already her engines had stopped, and the foam at her prow was dying away. One could see that a pilot was expected. Quite a crowd of people, even at that early hour, was gathered at the rail. A ladder of rope was hanging over the side, almost at the water's edge.

The little yawl bearing the pilot pulled square across the steamer's course. When the vessel drifted slowly up, the yawl nosed the great black side and drifted back by the ladder. One of the steamer's crew threw down a rope, which the oarsman of the yawl caught. This held the yawl still, close to the ladder, and the pilot, jumping for a good hold, began slowly to climb upward. No sooner had he seized the rope ladder than the engines started and the steamer moved off. The little yawl, left alone like a cork on a thrashing sea, headed toward us. The schooner tacked and came round in a half circle to pick it up, which was done with safety.

This was a busy morning. Before breakfast another ship had appeared, a tramp steamer, and a pilot was dressing to board her. Down the fore hatch could be seen the cook, frying potatoes and meat, and boiling coffee. The change in weather was pleasing to him, too, for he was singing as he clattered the dishes and set the table. In the cabin the pipes of the pilots were on, and the two old salts were at pinochle harder than ever.

Another pilot left before breakfast, and after he was gone another steamer appeared, this time the *Paris*. It looked as though we would soon lose all our pilots and have to return to New York. After the pilot had gone aboard the *Paris*, however, the wind died down and we sailed no more. Gradually the sea grew smoother, and we experienced a day of perfect idleness. Hour after hour the boat rocked like a cradle. Seagulls gathered around and dipped their wings in charming circles. Flocks of ducks passed northward in orderly flight, honking as they went. A little land-bird, a poor, bedraggled sparrow, evidently blown to sea by adverse winds, found rest and salvation in our rigging. Now it was perched upon the main boom, and now upon the guy of the gaff-topsail, but ever and anon, on this and the following day it could be seen, sometimes attempting to fly shoreward, but always returning after a fruitless quest for land. No vessel appeared, however. We merely rocked and waited.

The sailors in the forecastle told stories. The pilots in the rear talked New York politics and criminal mysteries. The cook brewed and baked. Night fell upon one of the fairest skies that it is given us earthlings to behold. Stars came out and blinked. The lightship at Sandy Hook cast a far beacon, but no steamer took another pilot that day.

Once during the watch that night it seemed that a

steamer far off to the southeastward was burning a blue light, the signal for a pilot. The man at the wheel scanned the point closely, then took a lighted torch made of cotton and alcohol and circled it slowly three times in the air. No answering blue light rewarded him. Another time there grew upon the stillness the far-off muffled sound of a steamer's engine. You could hear it distinctly, a faint "Pump, pump, pump, pump, pump." But no light could be seen. The signal torch was again waved, but without result. The distinct throb grew less and less, and finally died away. Some of the pilots commented as to this but could not explain it. They could not say why a vessel should travel without lights at night.

At midnight a little breeze sprang up and the schooner cruised about. In one direction appeared a faint glimmer, which when approached, proved to be the riding light of a freight steamer at anchor. All was still and dark aboard her, save for two or three red and yellow lights, which gleamed like sleepless eyes out of the black hulk. The man at the wheel called a sailor.

"Go forward, Johnnie," he said, "and hail her. See if she wants a pilot."

The man went to the prow and stood until the schooner drew quite near.

"Steamer, ahoy!" he bellowed.

No answer.

"Steamer, ahoy!" he called again. A light moved in the cabin of the other vessel. Finally a voice answered.

"Want a pilot?" asked our sailor.

"We have one," said the dim figure, and disappeared.

"Is it one of the pilots of your association that they have?" I asked.

"Yes; they couldn't have any other. They probably picked him up from one of our far-out boats. Every incoming steamer must take a pilot, you know. That's the law. All pilots belong to this one association. It's merely a question of our being around to supply them."

It turned out from his explanation that the desire of the pilots to get a steamer was merely to obtain their days off. When a pilot brings in a steamer it is not likely that he will be sent out again for three days. Each one puts in about the same number of days a month, and all get the same amount of pay. There is no rivalry for boats, and no loss of money by missing a steamer. If one boat misses her, another is sure to catch her farther in. If she refuses to take a pilot the Government compels her owners to pay a fine of fifty dollars, the price of a pilot to take her in.

On the third day now breaking we were destined to lose another pilot. It was one of the two inveterate pinochlers.

That night we anchored off Babylon, Long Island, in the stillest of waters. The crew spent the evening lounging in their bunks and reading, while the remaining pilots amused themselves as usual. Two of them engaged for a time in a half-hearted game of cards. One told stories, but with the departure of so many the spirits of the company drooped. There was no breeze. The flap-flap of the sails went on monotonously. Breakfast came, and then nine o'clock, and still we rocked in one spot. Then a steamer appeared. As usual, it was announced long before my untrained eyes could discern it. But, with the first word, the remaining valiant pinochler went below to pack. He was back in a few minutes, very much improved in spirits and appearance.

"Does she starboard any?" he asked the man at the wheel.

The latter used the telescope and then said:

"Don't seem to, sir."

"Think she sees us?"

"Can't tell, sir," said the boatman gravely.

"Spec' we'd better fire the gun, eh?"

"Yes, sir."

"You strip the gun. I'll take the wheel."

So a little gun—a tiny cannon, no less—was made ready and while it was being put in place at the lee rail, Germond, the oldest of the pilots, came on deck and took the wheel.

"Going to fire the gun, eh?" he observed, in deep bass tones.

"Yes," said the pinochler.

"Well, that's right. Blaze away."

The boatman, who had superintended the charging of the gun, now pulled a wire attached to a cap and the little cannon spat out a flame with a roar that shook the boat.

"Do they do this often?" I asked the footman.

"Not very. When fogs are on and boats can't find

us it comes in handy. There's hardly any use in this
case. I guess she sees us.''

Germond, at the wheel, seemed to enjoy playing war-
ship, for he called out: ''Fire again, Johnnie!''

''Won't she turn?'' asked the restless pinochler.

''Don't seem to.''

''Then,'' said he, and cast a droll look of derision
upon the midget cannon and the immense steamer,
''sink her!''

With the third shot, however, we could see the steamer
begin to turn, and in a little while she was headed toward
us. We could not move and so we waited, while the
anxious pinochler walked the deck. Long before she
was near he ordered the yawl ready, and when she was
yet three-quarters of a mile off, cast over and jumped
aboard. He seemed somewhat afraid the yawl would
not be seen, and so took along with him a pilot flag, which
was a square of blue cloth fastened to a long bamboo
pole. This he held aloft as the men rowed, and away
they went far over the green sea.

The cook served coffee at three, and was preparing
supper when another steamer was sighted. She came
up rapidly, a great liner from Gibraltar, with a large
company of Italians looking over the rail.

''No supper for you,'' said Germond. ''You'll have
to eat with the Dagos.''

''Oh, I don't mind,'' returned the other, smiling. ''I
want to get back to New York.''

Just before supper, and when the sun was crimsoning
the water in the west, a ''catspaw'' came up and filled

our sails. The boat moved slowly off. At supper Germond announced:

"Well, I go now."

"Is there a steamer?"

"No, but I go on the other pilot-boat. I see her over there. The last man always leaves his boat and goes on one with more men. That allows this boat to go back for another crew."

"Do you get the first steamer in, on the other boat?"

"Yes, I have the first turn." I understood now why our crew, at the outset, objected to any pilots being taken on our boat. It delayed the return of those on board to New York. "Steward!" called Germond, finally, "tell one of the men back there to run up a signal for the other boat."

"Ay! Ay! sir!" called back the steward.

At half after six the other pilot-boat drew near and Germond packed his sea clothes and came up on deck.

"Well, here she is, boys," he said. "Now I leave you."

They put out the yawl and he jumped in. When he had gone we watched him climbing aboard the other schooner.

"Now for New York!" exclaimed McLaughlin, the boatswain, and master of the crew in the absence of any pilot.

"Do we sail all night?"

"To get there by morning we'll have to."

All sails were then hoisted, and we bore away slowly. Darkness fell. The stars came out. Far away the revolving light of the Highlands of Navesink was our guide. Far behind, the little pilot-boat which had received Germond was burning a beacon for some steamer which had signaled a blue light. Gradually this grew more and more dim, and the gloom enveloped all.

We sat with subdued spirits at the prow, discussing the dangers of the sea. McLaughlin, who had been five years in the service, told of accidents and disappearances in the past. Once, out of the night had rushed a steamer, cutting a boat such as ours in two. One pilot-boat that had gone out two years ago had never returned. Not a stick or scrap was found to indicate what had become of her fifteen men. He told how the sounding of the fog-horns had chilled his heart the first year of his service, and how the mournful lapping of the waters had filled him with dread. And as we looked and saw nothing but blackness, and listened and heard nothing but the sipping of the still waters, it did seem as though the relentless sea merely waited its time. Some day it might have them all, sailor and cook, and where now were rooms and lockers would be green water and strange fishes.

That night we slept soundly. A fine wind sprang up, and when morning came we were scurrying home over a thrashing sea. We raced past Sandy Hook and put up the bay. By eight o'clock we were at the Narrows, with the Battery in sight. The harbor looked like a city of masts. After the lonely sea it seemed alive with a multitude of craft. Tugs went puffing by. Scows and steamers mingled. Amid so much life the sea seemed safe.

BUMS

WHENEVER I think of them I think of the spectacle
that genius of the burlesque world of my day, Nat Wills,
used to present when, in fluttering rags and tatters, his
vestless shirt open at the breast, revealing no underwear, his shoes three times too big, and torn and cracked,
a small battered straw hat, from a hole in which his
hair protruded, his trousers upheld by a string, and
that indefinable smirk of satisfaction of which he was
capable flickering over his dirty and unshaven face he
was wont to strike an attitude worthy of a flight of
oratory, and exclaim: "Fifteen years ago to-day I was
a poor, dispirited, broken-down tramp sitting on a bench
in a park, not a shirt to my back. Not a decent pair of
shoes on my feet. A hat with a hole in it. No money
to get a shave or a bath or a place to sleep. No place
to eat. Not a friend in the world to turn to. My torn
and frayed trousers held up by a string. Yet" (striking
his chest dramatically) "look at me now!" And then
he would lift one hand dramatically, as much as to
say, "Could any change be greater?"

The humor was not only in the contrast which his
words implied and his appearance belied, but in a certain definite and not unkindly characterization of the
bum as such, that smug and even defiant disregard of
the conventions and amenities which characterizes so

many of them and sets them apart as a species quite
distinct from the body social—for that they truly are.
And for that very reason they have always had a
peculiar interest for me, even a kind of fascination, such
as an arrestingly different animal might have for others.
And here in the great city, from time to time I have
encountered so many of them, suggesting not poverty or
want but a kind of devil-may-care indifference and even
contempt for all that society as we know it prizes so
highly—order, cleanliness, a job, a good suit of clothes,
marriage, children, respected membership in various
orders, religion, politics—anything and everything that
you will. And yet, by reason of their antithesis and
seeming antipathy to all this, interesting.

For, say what you will, it does take something that
is not social, and most certainly independent, either in
the form of thought or temperament, to permit one to
thus brazenly brave the notions and the moods, to say
nothing of the intellectual convictions, of those who
look upon the things above described as essential and
permanent. These astonishingly strange men, with their
matted hair over their eyes, their dirty skins, their
dirty clothes, their large feet encased in torn shoes, their
hats with holes in them and their hair actually protruding—just as though there were rules or conventions
governing them in the matter of dress. Along railroad tracks and roads outside the large cities of the country I have seen them (curiously enough, I have never
seen a woman tramp), singly or in groups, before a fire,
the accredited tin can at hand for water, a degenerate
pail brought from somewhere in which something is being

cooked over a fire. And on occasion, as a boy, I have found them asleep in the woods, under a tree, or in some improvised hole in a hay or straw stack, snoring loudly or resting as only the just and the pure in heart should rest.

But here in the great city I have always thought them a little strange and out of place. They consort so poorly with the pushing, eager, seeking throngs. And arrayed as they are, and as unkempt and unwashed, not even the low-priced lodging houses of the Bowery would receive them, and most certainly they would not pay the price of fifteen or twenty cents which would be required to house them, even if they had it. They are not of that kidney. And as for applying to a police station at any time, it were better that they did not. In bitter weather an ordinary citizen might do so with safety and be taken care of, but these, never. They would be driven out or sent to the Island, as the work-house here is called. Their principal lodging resource in times of wintry stress appears to be some grating covering a shaft leading to an engine room of some plant operative the night through, from which warm air pours; or some hallway in a public building, or the ultra-liberal and charitable lodging house of some religious mission. Quite often on an icy night I have seen not a few of them lying over the gratings of the subway at Fourteenth Street and at other less conspicuous points, where, along with better men than themselves, they were trusting to the semi-dry warm air that poured up through to prevent death from freezing. But the freeze being over, they would go their ways, I am sure, and never mend them from any fear of a like experience. And it is exactly that about them which has always interested me. For, by and large, I have never been able to feel that they either craved or deserved the need of that sympathy that we so freely extend to others of a less sturdy and different character. In truth, they are never as poor physically and nervously as many of those who, though socially fallen, yet appear to be better placed in the matter of clothes, food and mood. They are, in the main, neither lean nor dispirited, and they take life with too jaunty an air to permit one to be distressed about them. They remind me more of gulls or moles, or some different and unsocial animal that still finds in man his rightful prey or source of supply. And I am positive that theirs is a disposition, either inherited or made so by circumstances, which has not too much chemic opposition to their lackadaisical state, that prefers it even to some other forms of existence. Summer or winter I have seen them here and there, in the great city, but never in those poorer neighborhoods, frequented by those who are really in need, and always with the air of physical if not material comfort hovering about them, and that in the face of garments that would better become an ashcan than a man. The rags. The dirt. And yet how often of a summer's evening have I not seen them on the stones of doorways and the planks of docks and lumber yards, warm and therefore comfortable, resting most lazily and snoring loudly, as though their troubles or irritations, whatever they were, were far from them.

And in these same easier seasons have I not seen
them making their way defiantly or speculatively among
the enormous crowds on the principal streets of the
city, gazing interestedly and alertly into the splendid
shopwindows, and thinking what thoughts and contemplating what prospects! It is not from these that
the burglars are recruited or the pickpockets, as the
police will tell you. And the great cities do not ordinarily attract them; though they come, occasionally,
drawn, I suppose, by the hope of novelty, and interested,
quite as is Dives in Egypt or India, by what they see.
Now and then you will behold one, as have I, being
"ragged" by one of those idle mischievous gangs of the
city into whose heartless clutches he has chanced to fall.
His hat will be seized and pulled or crushed down over
his eyes, his matted hair or beard pulled, straws or rags
or paper shoved between his back and his coat and himself made into a veritable push-ball or punching-bag to
be shoved here and there, before he is allowed to depart.
And for no offense other than that he is as he is. Yet
whether they are spiritually outraged or depressed by
this I would not be able to say. To me they have ever
appeared to be immune to what would spiritually degrade
and hence torture and depress another.

Their approach to life, if anything, appears to be
one of hoyden contempt for conventional processes of
all kinds, a kind of parasitic indifference to anything
save their own comfort, joined with a not unadmirable
love for the out-of-doors and for change. So often, as
I have said, I have seen them about the great city,

asleep in the cool recesses of not-much-frequented doors and passageways, and in lumberyards and odd corners, anywhere where they were not likely to be observed. And my observation of them has led me to conclude that they do not feel and hence do not suffer as do other and more sensitive men. They are not interested in material prosperity as such, and they will not work. If any one has ever seen one with that haunted look which at times characterizes the eye of those who take life and society so desperately and seriously, and that betokens one whom life is able to torture, I have yet to hear of it.

But what an interesting and amazing spectacle they present, and what amusing things are to be related of them! I personally have seen a group of such rowdies, such as characterize some New York street corners even to this day pouring wood-alcohol on one of these fellows whom they chanced to find asleep, and then setting fire to it in order to observe what would be the effect of the discovery by the victim of himself in flames. And subsequently pursuing him down the street with shouts and ribald laughter. On another occasion, in Hudson Street, the quondam home of the Hudson Dusters, I have seen six or eight of such youths pushing another one such about, carrying him here and there by the legs and arms and tossing him into the air above an old discarded mattress, until an irate citizen, not to be overawed himself, and of most respectable and God-fearing mien, chose to interfere and bring about a release. And in another part of this same good city, that part of the waterfront which lies east of South Ferry and south

of Fulton Street, I have seen one such most persistently
and thoroughly doused by as many as ten playful wags,
all in line, yet at different doors, and each discharging
a can or a bucket of water upon the fleeing victim, who
sought to elude them by running. But, following this
individual to see what his mood might be, I could not
see that he had taken the matter so very much to heart.
Once free of his pursuers, he made his way to a dock,
where, seated behind some boxes in the sun, he made
shift to dry himself and rest without appearing to fret
over what had occurred.

On one occasion I remember standing on the forward
end of a ferry boat that once plied between New York
and Jersey City, the terminal of one of the great railways entering the city, when one of these peculiar creatures took occasion to make his very individual point
of view clear. It was late afternoon, and the fore-
runners of the homeward evening rush of commuters
were already beginning to appear. He was dirty and
unkempt and materially degraded as may be, but not at
all cast down or distrait. On the contrary. Having
been ushered to the dock by a stalwart New York policeman and put on board and told never to return on pain
of arrest, he was still in an excellent mood in regard to
it all. Heigh-ho! The world was not nearly so bad as
many made out. His toes sticking out, the ragged ends
of his coat flapping about him, a wretched excuse for a
hat on his head, he still trotted here and there, a genial
and knowing gleam in his eye, to say nothing of a Mona
Liza-like leer about his mouth. He surveyed us all,

kempt and worthy exemplars of the proprieties, with the air of one who says: "Well, well! Such decent and such silly people. All sheep who know only the conventional ways and limitations of the city and nothing else, creatures who look on me as a wastrel, a failure and a ne'er-do-well. Nevertheless, I am not as hopeless or as hapless as they think, the sillies." And to make this clear he strode defiantly to and fro, smirking now on one and now on another, and coming near to one and again to another, thereby causing each and every one to retreat for the very simple reason that the odor of him was as unconventional as himself.

Finding himself thus evaded and rather scorned for this procedure, he retired to the forward part of the deck for a time and communed with himself; but not for long. For, deciding after all, I presume, that this was a form of defeat and that he was allowing himself to be unduly put upon or outplaced, at least, by conventionalists, for whom he had absolutely no respect, he whirled, and surveying the assembled company of commuters who had by now gathered in a circle about him, like sheep surveying some unwonted spectacle, he waved one hand dramatically and announced: "I'm a dirty, drunken, blue-nosed bum, and I don't give a damn! See? See? I don't give a damn!" and with that he caroled a little tune, whistled, twiddled his fingers at all of us, did a light gay step here and there, and then, lifting his torn coat-tails, shook them defiantly and contemptuously in the face of all of us.

There were of course a few terrified squeaks from a

few horrified and sanctified maidens, old and young, who retreated to the protection of the saloon behind. There were also dark and reproving frowns from a number of solid and substantial citizens, very well-dressed indeed, who pretended not to notice or who even frowned on others for noticing. Incidentally, there were a few delighted and yet repressed squeals from various youths and commonplace nobodies, like myself, and eke a number of heavy guffaws from more substantial citizens of uncertain origin and who should have, presumably, known better.

Yet, after all, as I told myself, afterward, there was considerable to be said for the point of view of this man, or object. It was at least individual, characterful and forceful. He was, decidedly, out of step with all those about him, but still in step, plainly, with certain fancies, moods, conditions more suited to his temperament. Decidedly, his point of view was that of the box-car, the railroad track, the hay-pile and the roadside. But what of it? Must one quarrel with a crow for being a crow, or with a sheep for being a sheep? Not I.

And in addition, to prove that he really did not care a damn, and that his world was his own, once the gates were lifted he went dancing off the boat and up the dock, a jaunty, devil-may-care air and step characterizing him, and was soon lost in the world farther on. But about it all, as it seemed to me, there was something that said to those of us who were left in the way, that he and his kind were neither to be pitied nor blamed. They were as they were, unsocial, unconventional, indifferent to the saving, grasping, scheming plans of men, and in accord with moods if not plans of their own. They will not, and I suspect cannot, run with the herd, even if they would. And no doubt they taste a form of pleasure and satisfaction that is as grateful to them as are all the moods and emotions which characterize those who are so unlike them and who see them as beings so utterly to be pitied or foresworn. At least I imagine so.

THE MICHAEL J. POWERS ASSOCIATION

In an area of territory including something like forty thousand residents of the crowded East Side of New York there dwells and rules an individual whose political significance might well be a lesson to the world.

Stout, heavy-headed and comfortably constituted, except in the matter of agility, he walks; and where he is not a personal arbiter he is at least a familiar figure. Not a saloon-keeper (and there is one to every half-block) but knows him perfectly and would be glad to take off his hat to him if it were expected, and would bring him into higher favor. Not a street cleaner or street division superintendent, policeman or fireman but recognizes him and goes out of his way to greet him respectfully. Store-keepers and school children, the basement barber and the Italian coal-dealer all know who is meant when one incidentally mentions "the boss." His progress, if one might so term his daily meanderings, is one of continual triumph. It is not coupled with huzzahs, it is true, but there is a far deeper and more vital sentiment aroused, a feeling of reverence due a master.

I have in mind a common tenement residence in a crowded and sometimes stifling street in this vicinity, where at evening the hand-organs play and the children run the thoroughfare by thousands. Poor, compact; rich only in those quickly withering flowers of flesh and

44

blood, the boys and girls of the city. It is a section from which most men would flee when in search of rest and quiet. The carts and wagons are numerous, the people are hard-working and poor. Stale odors emanate from many hallways and open windows.

Yet here, winter and summer, when evening falls and the cares of his contracting business are over for the day, this individual may be seen perched upon the front stoop of his particular tenement building or making a slow, conversational progress to the clubhouse, a half-dozen doors to the west. So peculiar is the political life of the great metropolis that his path for this short distance is blockaded by dozens who seek the awesome confessional of his ear.

"Mr. Powers, if you don't mind, when you're through I would like a word with you."

"Mr. Powers, if you're not too busy, I want to ask you a question."

"Mr. Powers—" how often is this simple form of request made into his ear. Three hours' walking, less than three hundred feet—this tells the story of the endless number that seek to buttonhole him. "Rubbing something offen him," is the way the politicians interpret these conversations.

Being a big man with a very "big" influence, he is inclined to be autocratic, an attitude of mind which endless whispered pleas are little calculated to modify. Always he carries himself with a reserved and secret air. There is something uncompromising about the wide mouth, with its long upper lip, the thin line of the lips set like the edge of an oyster shell, the square, heavily-

weighted jaw beneath, which is cold and hard. Yet his
mouth is continually wrinkling at the corners with the
semblance of a smile, and those nearest as well as those
farthest from him will tell you that he has a good heart.
You may take that with a grain of salt, or not, as you
choose.

I had not been in the district very long before I
saw in the windows of nearly every kind of store a
cheaply-printed placard announcing that the annual
outing of the Michael J. Powers Association would take
place on Tuesday, August 2d, at Wetzel's Grove, Col-
lege Point. The steamer *Cygnus,* leaving Pier 30, East
River, would convey them. Games, luncheon and dinner were to be the entertainment. Tickets five dollars.

Any one who has ever taken even a casual glance at
the East Side would be struck by the exorbitance of
such a charge as five dollars. No one would believe for
an instant that these saving Germans, Jews and other
types of hardworking nationalities would willingly in-
vest anything over fifty cents in any such outing. Times
are always hard here, the size of a dollar exceedingly
large. Yet there was considerable stir over the pros-
pective pleasure of the day in this district.

"Toosday is a great day," remarked my German
barber banteringly, when I called on the Saturday
previous to get shaved.

"What about Tuesday?"

"Mr. Powers holds his picnic. Der will be some beer
drunk, you bet."

"What do you know about it? Do you belong to
the association?"

"Yes. I was now six years a member alretty. It is a fine association."

"What makes them charge five dollars? There can't be very many around here who can afford to pay that much."

"Der will be t'ree t'ousand, anyway," he answered, "maybe more. Efferybody goes. Mr. Powers say 'Go,' den dey go."

"Oh, Mr. Powers makes you go, does he?"

"No," he replied conservatively. "It is a nice picnic. We haf music, a cubble of bands. Der is racing, schwimming, all de beer you want for nodding, breakfast und dinner, a nice boat ride. Oh, we haf a good time."

"Do you belong to Tammany?"

"No, sir."

"Hold any office under Mr. Powers?"

"No, sir."

"Well, why do you go, then? There must be some reason."

"I haf de polling place in my back room," he finally admitted.

"How much do you get for that?"

"Sixty-five dollars a year."

"And you give five of that back for a ticket?"

He smiled, but made no reply.

It was on Monday that the German grocer signified his intention of going.

"Do all of you people have to attend?" I inquired.

"No," he replied, "we don't have to. There will be

somebody there from most of the stores around here, though.''

"Why?"

"Ask Mr. Powers. There'll be somebody there from every saloon, barbershop, restaurant and grocery in the district.''

"But why?''

"Ho,'' he returned, "it's a good picnic. Mr. Powers looks mighty fine marching at the head. They say he is next after Croker now.''

Among the petty dealers of the neighborhood generally could be found the same genial acceptance of the situation.

"Dat is a great parade,'' said a milk dealer to me. "You will see somet'ing doing if you are in de distric' dat night. Senators walk around just de same as street cleaners; police captains, too.''

I thought of the condescension of these high-and-mighties deigning to walk with the common street cleaners, coerced into line.

"Are you going?'' I asked.

"Yes.''

"Want to go?''

"Oh, it's good enough.''

"What do you think of Powers?''

"He is a great man. Stands next to Croker. Wait till you see de procession dat goes by here.''

This was the point, the procession. Any such rich material evidence of power was a sufficient reason for

loyalty in the minds of these people. They worship
power. None know it better than these particular individuals who lead them. The significance of forcing so
many to march, coming thus rapidly home to me, I
dropped around to the district Tammany club on the
afternoon and evening preceding this eventful day.
The palatial chambers of the district leader in the club
are his arena, and on this particular evening these same
were the center of much political activity. Signs of the
power of which I had heard and seen other evidences
were here renewed before my eyes. Arranged in a
great meeting-chamber, the political hall of the club,
were tables and counters, behind which were standing
men who, as I learned immediately afterward, were of
high standing in the district and city organization.
Deputy commissioners of the water department, the
department of highways, of sewers; ex-State senators,
ex-assemblymen, police sergeants, detective sergeants,
aldermen, were all present and all doing yeoman service.
Upon the tables were immense sheets, yards in
diameter, with lists of names. Back of the tables were
immense piles of caps, badges and canes. As fast as
the owners of the names on the list appeared their
names were checked and their invitation cards, which
they threw down cheerily upon the table in company
with a five-dollar bill, were marked paid and passed
back for further use. At the other tables these cards
were then good for a cap, a cane, and two badges, all
of which the members were expected to wear.
Energetic as were the half-dozen deputy commis-

sioners, police sergeants, detective sergeants, ex-assemblymen and the like, who labored at this clerical task without coats or vests, they were no match for the throng of energetic Tammanyites who filed in and out, carrying their hats and canes away with them. Hundreds of clerks, precinct captains, wardmen, streetcleaners, two-thousand-dollar-a-year clerks, swarmed the spacious lobby and greeted one another in that perfunctory way so common to most political organizations. The "Hellos," "Well, old mans," "Well, how are things?" and "There goes" were as thick and all-pervading as the tobacco smoke which filled the rooms. Tammanyites in comfortable positions of all degrees moved about in new clothes and squeaky shoes. Distinct racial types illustrated how common is the trait of self-interest and how quick are the young Germans, Irish and Jews to espouse some cause or profession where self-interest and the simultaneous advancement of the power of some particular individual or organization are not incompatible. Smilingly they greeted one another, with that assumption of abandon and good fellowship which was as evidently assumed for the occasion as could be. In the case of many it was all too plain that it was an effort to be as bright and genial as they appeared to be. However, they had mastered the externals and could keep a straight face. How hard those straight mouths could become, how defiant those narrow protruding jaws, only time and a little failure on some one's part would tell.

While the enthusiasm of this labor was at its highest

Mr. Powers put in an appearance. He was as pictured. On this occasion, his clothes were plain black, his necktie black, his face a bright red, partially due to a recent, and very close shave. He moved about with catlike precision and grace, and everywhere politicians buttonholed or bowed to him, the while he smiled upon every one in the same colorless, silent and decidedly secret way.

"Mr. Powers, we're going to run out of caps before long," one official hurried forward to say.

"Dugan has that in charge," he replied.

"I guess we'll have a full attendance," whispered another of those high in his favor.

"That's good."

While he was sitting in his rosewood-finished office at one side of the great room dozens of those who had come from other districts to pay their respects and buy a ticket looked in upon him.

"I'll be with you in the morning, Michael," said a jolly official from another district.

"Thank you, George," he replied smiling. "We'll have a fine day, I hope."

"I hope so," said the other.

Sitting about in their chairs, some of the older officials who had come to the club on this very special occasion fell into a reflective mood and dug up the conditions of the past.

"Do you remember Mike as an alderman, Jerry?"

"I do. There was none better."

"Remember his quarrel with Murtha?"

"Aye! He was for taking no odds from anybody those days."

"Brave as a lion, he was."

"He was."

"There's no question of his nerve to-day."

"None at all."

"He's a good leader."

"He is."

"How did Powers ever come to get his grip upon the district?" I inquired of an old office-holder who was silently watching the buzzing throng in the rooms before him.

"He was always popular with the boys," he answered. "Long before the fortieth was ever divided he was popular with the boys of one section of it. Creamer was leader at that time."

"Yes, but how did he get up?"

"How does anybody get up?" he returned. "He worked up. When he was assistant mechanic in the Fire Department, getting a hundred and twenty a month, he gave half of it away. Anybody could get money off him; that was the trouble. I've known him as a lad to give seventy-seven dollars away in one month."

"Who was he, that he should distribute money so freely?"

"Captain of two hundred, of course. He wasn't called upon to spend his own money, though."

"And that started him?"

"He was always a smart fellow," returned the speaker. "Creamer liked him. Creamer was a fighter himself. Mike was as brave as a lion. When they divided the district he got John Kelly to give Powers the other half. He did it, of course, because he could trust Powers to stand with him. But he did it, just the same.''

"Kelly was head of Tammany Hall then?''

"He was.''

While we were talking a cart-driver or street-cleaner made his way through the broad street-door towards the private office where so many others were, taking off his hat as he did so and waiting respectfully to one side. Dozens of young politicians were trifling about. The deputy commissioner of highways, the assistant deputy tax commissioner, the assistant deputy of the department of sewers, and others were lounging comfortably in the chief's room. Three or four black-suited, priestly-looking assistants from the office of the chief of police were conferring in that wise, subtle and whispering way which characterizes all the conversation of those numerous aspirants for higher political preferment.

Some one stalked over to the waiting newcomer and said: "Well?''

"Is Mr. Powers here this evening?''

At the sound of his name the leader, who was lounging in his Russia-leather chair within, raised his head, and seeing the figure in the reception area, exclaimed:

"Put on your hat, old man! No one is expected to put off his hat here. Come right in!''

He paused, and as the street-sweeper approached he turned lightly to his satellites. "Get the hell out of here, now, and let this man have a chance," he said quickly, the desire to be genial with all being apparent. The deputies came out of the room smiling and the old man was ushered in.

"Now, Mr. Cassidy," I heard him begin, but slowly he moved around to the door and closed it. The conversation was terminated so far as we listeners from without were concerned. Only the profuse bowing of the old man as he came out, the "Thank ye, Mr. Powers, thank ye," repeated and repeated, gave any indication as to what the nature of the transaction might have been.

While such incidents were passing the evening for some, the great crowd of ticket-purchasers continued. Hundreds upon hundreds filed in and out, some receiving a nod, some a mere glance of recognition, some only a scrutiny of a very peculiar sort.

"Are these all members of the club?" I asked of a friend, an ex-assemblyman and now precinct captain in the block in which I voted.

"They're nearly all members of the district organization," he replied.

"How many votes do you claim to control?"

"About five thousand."

"How many votes are there in the district?"

"Ten thousand."

"Then you have fully half the votes assured before election-time rolls around?"

"We've got to have," he replied significantly. "There's no going into a fight under Powers, unless he knows where the votes are. He won't stand for it."

While sitting thus watching the proceedings, the hours

passed and the procession thinned down to a mere handful. By midnight it looked as if all were over, and the leader came forth and quietly took his leave.

"Anything more, Eddie?" he asked of a peaked-face young Irishman outside his office door.

"Nothing that I can think of."

"You'll see to the building?" he asked the deputy commissioner of taxes.

"It'll look like a May party in the morning, Chief."

THE FIRE

IT is two o'clock of a sultry summer afternoon in one of those amazingly crowded blocks on the East Side south of Fourteenth Street, which is drowsing out its commonplace existence through the long and wearisome summer. The men of the community, for it may as well be called a community since it involves all that makes a community, and that in a very small space, are away at work or in their small stores, which take up all of the ground floors everywhere. The housewives are doing their shopping in these same stores—groceries, bakeries, meat and fish markets. From the streets which bound this region people are pouring through, a busy host, coming from what sections of the city and the world and going to what sections of the city and the world no one may divine. Wagons rattle, trucks rumble by with great, creaking loads, a slot conduit trolley puts a clattering car past every fifteen or twenty seconds. The riffraff of life fills it as full as though it were the center of the world. Children, since there is no school now, are playing here. The streets are fairly alive with a noisy company of urchins who play at London Bridge and My Love's Lover, and are constantly getting in the way of one another and of every one else who chances to pass this way.

Suddenly, in the midst of an almost wearisome peace,

comes the cry of fire. It comes from the cleanly depths
of Number 358, in the middle of this block, where one
Frederick Halsmann, paint-dealer and purveyor of useful oils to the inhabitants of this neighborhood, has
apparently been busy measuring out a gallon of gasoline.
He has been doing a fairly thriving business here for
years, the rejuvenation of a certain apartment district
nearby having brought him quite a demand for explosive
and combustible oils, such as naphtha, gasoline and ben-
zine, to say nothing of turpentine and some other less
dangerous products, all of which he has stored in his
basement. There is a law against keeping more than
twenty gallons of any kind of explosive oil in a store
or the basement of a store, but this law, like so many
others of the great city, enjoys its evasions. What is
the law between friends?

All the same, and at last, a fire has broken out—no
one ever knows quite how. A passing stranger notes
smoke issuing from a grating in front of the store. He
calls the attention of Mr. Halsmann to it, but even before
that the latter has seen it. He starts to descend an
outside stairway leading to his particular basement but
is halted by a terrific explosion which knocks him and
some strangers down, shatters the windows in his own
and other stores four or five numbers away, and tears
a hole in the floor of his store through which his paints, a
counter, a cash register and some other things begin to
tumble. He is too astounded to quite grasp it all but
recovering his feet he begins to shout: "Maria! Maria!
Come quick! And the children! Come out! Come
down!"

But his cries come too late. He has scarcely got the
words out of his mouth when a second explosion, far
more violent than the first, tears up the floor and the
stairs leading to his home and throws the lurid fire
into the rooms above. It smashes the glass in the front
windows of stores across the street and blows a perfect
hurricane of fire in the same direction. People run, yell-
ing and screaming, a hundred voices raising the cry of
"Fire!"

"My God! My God!" cries an old Jewish butcher
over the way. He is standing in front of his store
wringing his hands. "It is Halsmann's store! Run
quick!" This to a child near him. Then he also runs.
An idle policeman breaks for the nearest fire alarm box,
and the crowds of the neighboring thoroughfares surge
in here until the walks and the paving stones are black
with people. A hundred heads pop out of neighboring
windows. A thousand voices take up the cry of "Fire!"

From the houses adjoining, and even in this one, for
the upper floors have not yet been completely shattered,
people are hurrying. A woman with a child on the
third floor is screaming and waving her free hand frantically. A score of families in the adjoining buildings
are gathering their tawdry valuables together and
hastening into the street. Some policemen from neighboring beats, several from the back rooms of saloons,
come running, and the fight to obtain a little order in
anticipation of the fire engines begins.

"Get back there!" commands Officer Casey, whose
one idea of natural law in a very unspiritual world is
that all policeman should always be in front where

they can see best. He begins pushing hard at the vitals
of a slender citizen whose curiosity is out of all pro-
portion to his strength. "Get back, I say! Ye'd think
ye owned the earth, the way ye're shovin' in here. Get
back!"

"Give 'em a cracк over the sconce," advises Officer
Rooney, who can see no use in wasting time bandying
words. "Back with ye! I'll not be tellin' ye twice.
Back!" And he places a brawny shoulder so as to do
the utmost damage in the matter of crushing bones. It is
rather good fun for a policeman who only a moment
before was wondering what to do with his time.

In the meanwhile the flames are sweeping upward. In
the basement, where gasoline sat by kerosene, and
naphtha by that, the urge of the flames is irresistible.
Already one small barrel and a five-gallon measure of
gasoline have gone, sacrificing to its concentrated force
the lives of Halsmann's wife and child. Now, a large
half-barrel having been reached, the floors to the third
level are ripped out by a terrifying crash that shatters
the panes of glass in the windows in the next block and
Plumber Davidson, on the third floor of the house next
door, running to get his pocketbook out of a kitchen
drawer and a kit of tools he had laid down before putting
his head out of the front window, is seen to be caught and
pinioned, and slaughtered where he stands. Street-
sweeper Donnelson's wife, a stout slattern of a woman,
who had run with many agonized exclamations to a
cradle to pick up her little round-headed Johnnie and
then to the mantel to grab a new clock, is later found in
the basement of the same building, caught midway be-

tween the iron railing of a stair and a timber. Mrs. Steinmetz, the Jewish peddler's wife, of the fourth floor, is blown to the ceiling from her kitchen floor, and then, tumbling down, left unconscious on a stretch of planking, from which later she is rescued.

Outside, on the ground below, the people are gazing in terror and intense satisfaction. Here is a spectacle for you, if you please, here the end of a dull routine of many days. The fire-god has broken loose. The demon flame is trying his skill against the children of men and the demon water. He has caught them unawares. He has seized upon the place where the best of their ammunition is stored. From his fortress in the cellar he is hurling huge forks of flame and great gusts of heat. Before him now men and women stand helpless. White-faced onlookers gaze upward with expressions of mingled joy and pain.

Clang! Clang! Clang!

And the wail of a siren.

And yet another.

And yet another.

They announce the men of the Fortieth Hook and Ladder Company, of the Twenty-seventh Hook and Ladder and Fire Patrol, of the Thirty-third Engine and Hook and Ladder Company, and the Fifty-first Engine and Hose Company, down through a long list of stations covering an area of a half-dozen square miles.

In the midst of the uproar about the burning building, the metallic cry of this rescuing host is becoming more and more apparent. From every section they come, the glistening surfaces of their polished vehicles and implements shining in the sun, the stacks of their engines issuing volumes of smoke. Fire boxes drop fiery sparks as they speed past neighboring corners, the firemen stoking as they come. Groups of hook-and-ladder handlers are unhooking and making ready their ladders. Others, standing upright on their careening vehicles, are adjusting rubber coats and making ready to invade the precincts of danger at once. The art of balancing on one foot while tugging at great coils of hose that are being uncoiled from speeding vehicles is being deftly illustrated. These men like this sort of thing. It is something to do. They are trained men, ready to fight the fire demon at a moment's notice, and they are going about their work with the ease and grace of those who feel the show as well as the importance of that which they do. Once more, after days of humdrum, they are the center of a tragedy, the cynosure of many eyes. It is exhilarating thus to be gazed at, as any one can see. They swing down from their machines in front of this holocaust with the nonchalance of men going to a dinner.

And the police reserves, they are here now too. This indifferent block, so recently the very heart of hum-drum, is now the center of a great company of policemen. The regular width of the street from side to side and corner to corner has been cleared and is now really parked off by policemen pushing back the gaping and surging throng. There are cries of astonishment as the onrushing flames leap now from building to build-ing, shouts of "Stay where you are!" to helpless women and children standing in open windows from which the smoke is threatening to drive them; there are great, wave-like pushings forward and recedings, as the officers, irritated by the eagerness of the crowd, endeavor to hold it in check.

"McGinnity and six men to the roof of 354!" comes the bellowing cry of a megaphone in the hands of a battalion chief.

"Hennessy and Company H, spread out the life net!"

"Williams! Williams! You and Dubo scale the walls quick! Get that woman above there! Turn your hose on there, Horton, turn your hose on! Where is Company B? Can't you people get in line for the work here?"

The assurance of the firemen, so used to the petty blazes that could be extinguished in half an hour by the application of a stream or two of water, has been slightly shaken by the evidence of the explosive nature of the material stored in the basement of this building. The sight of people hurrying from doorways with their few little valuables gathered up in trembling arms, or screaming in windows from which the flames and smoke have fairly shut off rescue, is, after all, disconcerting to the bravest. While the last explosion is shooting upward and outward and flames from the previously ignited ones are bursting through the side walls of adjoining structures and cutting off escape for a score, the firemen are loosing ladders and hose from a dozen still rolling vehicles and setting about the task of rescuing the victims. Suddenly a cask of kerosene, heated to the boiling point in the seething cauldron of the cellar, explodes, throwing a shower of blazing oil aloft which descends as a rain of fire. Over the crowd it pours, a licking, death-dealing rain, which sends them plunging madly away. In the rush, women and children are trampled and more than one over-ambitious sight-seer is struck by a falling dab of flaming oil. A police captain, standing in the middle of the street, is caught by a falling shower and instantly ignited. An old Polish Jew, watching the scene from the door of his eight-by-ten shop, is caught on the hand and sent crying within. Others run madly with burning coats and blazing hats, while over the roofs and open spaces can be seen more of these birdlike flames of fire fluttering to their destructive work in the distance. The power of the fire demon is at its height.

And now the servants of the water demon, the firemen, dismayed and excited, fall back a pace, only to return and with the strength of water at their command assail the power of the fire again. Streams of water are now spouting from a score of nozzles. A group of eight firemen, guided by a rotund battalion chief who is speaking through a trumpet, ascends the steps of a nearby doorway and gropes its way through the dark halls to apartments where frightened human beings may be cowering, too crazed by fear to undertake to rescue themselves. Another group of eight is to be seen working its way with scaling ladders to the roof of another building. They carry ropes which they hang over the eaves, thus constructing a means of egress for those who are willing and hardy enough to lay hold and descend in this fashion. Still another group of eight is spreading a net into which hovering, fear-crazed victims calling from windows above are commanded to jump. Through it all the regular puffing of the engines, the muffled voices of the captains shouting, and the rattling beat of the water as it plays upon the walls and batters its way through the windows and doors, can be heard as a monotone, the chorus of this grand contest in which man seeks for mastery over an element.

And yet the fire continues to burn. It catches a dressmaker who has occupied the rear rooms of the third floor of the building, two doors away from that of the paint-dealer's shop, and while she is still waving frantically for aid she is enveloped with a glorious golden shroud of fire which hides her completely. It rushes to where a lame flower-maker, Ziltman, is groping agonizedly before his windows on the fifth floor of another tenement, and sends into his nostrils a volume of thick smoke which smothers him entirely. It sends long streamers of flame licking about doorposts and window frames of still other buildings, filling stairways and area-landings with great dark clouds of vapor and bursting forth in lurid, sinister flashes from nooks and corners where up to now fire has not been suspected. It appears to be an all-devouring Nemesis, feeding as a hungry lion upon this ruck of wooden provender and this wealth of human life. The bodies of stricken human beings are but fuel for it—but small additions to its spirals of smoke and its tongues of flame.

And yet these battalions of fighters are not to be discouraged. They guess this element to be a blind one, indifferent alike to failure or success. It may rage on and consume the whole city. It may soon be compelled

to slink back to a smoldering heap. It appears to
desire to burn fiercely, and yet they know that it will
give way before its logical foe. Upon it, now, they are
heaping a score of streams, beating at distant windows,
tearing out distant doors, knocking the bricks from their
plastered places, of houses not on fire at all and so
setting up a barrier between it and other buildings,
destroying in fact the form and order of years in order
to make a common level upon which its enemy, water,
can meet and defeat it.

But these little ants of beings, how they have scurried before this battle royal between these two elements!
How fallen! How harried and bereft and tortured they
seem! Under these now blackened and charred timbers
and fallen bricks and stones and twisted plates of iron
are not a few of them, dead. And beyond the still
tempestuous battlefield, where flame and water still
fight, are thousands more of them, agape with wonder
and fear and pity. They do not know what water is,
nor fire. They only know what they do, how dangerous
they are, how really deadly and how indifferent to their
wishes or desires. Forefend! forefend! is the wisest
thought that comes to them, else these twain, and other
strange and terrible things like them, will devour us all.

But these elements. Here they are and here they
continue to battle until a given quantity of water has
been able to overcome a given amount of fire. Like the
fabled battle between the Efrit and the King's daughter,
they have fought each other over rooftops and in cellars
and in the very air, where flame and water meet, and
under twisted piles of timber and iron and stone.

Wherever any of the snaky heads of the demon fire have shown themselves, the flattened gusts of the demon water have assailed them. The two have fought in crevices where no human hand could reach. They have grappled with one another in titanic writhings above the rooftops, where the eyes of all men could see. They have followed one another to unexpected depths, fire showing itself wherever water has neglected to remain, the water returning where the fire has begun its battling anew. They have chased and twisted and turned, until at last, out-generaled in this instance, fire has receded and water conquered all.

But the petty little creatures who have been the victims of their contest, the chance occupants of the field upon which they chose to battle. But look at them now, agape with wonder and terror. And how they scurried! How jumped from the windows into nets, how clambered like monkeys down ladders, how gropingly they have staggered through halls of smoke, thick, rich smoke, as dark and soft and smooth as the fleece of a ram and as deadly as death.

And now small men, shocked by all that has befallen, gather and congratulate themselves on their victory or meditate on and bemoan their losses. The terror of it all!

"I say, John," says the battalion chief of the second division to the battalion chief of the first, "that was something of a fire, eh?"

"It was that," agrees the latter, looking grimly from under the rim of his wet red helmet.

"That Dutchman must have had a half-dozen barrels

of naphtha or gasoline down there to cause such a blow-up as that. Why, that last blast, just before I got here, sent the roof off, they tell me.''

"It did that," returns the other thoughtfully. "There'll be a big rumpus about it in the papers to-morrow. They ought to inspect these places better.''

"That's right. Well, he got his fill. His wife's down there now, I think, and his baby. He ain't been seen since the first explosion.''

"Too bad. But they oughtn't to do such things. They know the danger of it. Still, you never can tell 'em nothin'.''

THE CAR YARD

IF I were a painter one of the first things I would paint would be one or another of the great railroad yards that abound in every city, those in New York and Chicago being as interesting as any. Only I fear that my brush would never rest with one portrait. There would be pictures of it in sunshine and cloud, in rain and snow, in light and dark, and when heat caused the rails and the cars to bake and shimmer, and the bitter cold the mixture of smoke and steam to ascend in tall, graceful, rhythmic plumes that appear to be composed of superimposed circles and spirals of smoke and mist.

The variety of the cars. The variety of their contents. The long distances and differing climates and countries from which they have come—the Canadian snows, the Mexican uplands, Florida, California, Texas and Maine. As a boy, in the different cities and towns in which our family dwelt, I was forever arrested by the spectacle of these great freight trains, yellow, white, red, blue, green, toiling through or dissipating themselves in some terminal maze of tracks. I was always interested to note how certain cars, having reached their destination, would be sidetracked and left, and then presently the consignee or his agent or expressman would appear and the car be opened. Ice, potatoes, beef, furniture, machinery, boxed shipments of all kinds, would be taken out by some lone worker who, having

come with a wagon, would back it up to the opened door
and remove the contents. Most interesting of all to
me were the immense shipments of live stock, the pigs,
sheep, steers, on their last fatal journey and looking so
non-understandingly out upon the strange world in
which they found themselves, and baa-ing or moo-ing or
squealing in tones that gave evidence of the uncertainty,
the distress and the wonder that was theirs.

For a time in Chicago, between my eighteenth and
nineteenth years, I was employed as a car-tracer in one
of the great freight terminals of a railroad entering
Chicago, a huge, windy, forsaken realm far out on
the great prairie west of the city and harboring literally
a thousand or more cars. And into it and from it would
move such long freight trains, heavy with snow occasionally, or drenched with rain, and presenting such a
variety of things in cars: coal, iron, cattle, beef, which
would here be separated and entangled with or disentangled from many others and then moved on again in
the form of other long trains. The clanging engine
bells, the puffing stacks, the arresting, colorful brake-
men and trainmen in their caps, short, thick coats,
dirty gloves, and with their indispensable lanterns over
their arms. In December and January, when the days
were short and the nights fell early, I found myself with
long lists of car numbers, covering cars in transit and
concerning which or their contents owners or shippers
were no doubt anxious, hurrying here and there, now
up and down long tracks, or under or between the
somber cars that lined them, studying by the aid of my
lantern the tags and car numbers, seeing if the original

labels or addresses were still intact, whether the seals
had remained unbroken, on what track the car was, and
about where, and checking these various items on the
slip given me, and, all being correct, writing O. K. across
the face of it all. Betimes I would find a consigned car
already in place on some far sidetrack, the consignee
having already been notified, and some lone worker with
a wagon busily removing the contents. Sometimes, being
in doubt, I would demand to see the authorization, and
then report. But except for occasional cars, that however accurately billed never seemed to appear, no other
thing went wrong.

Subsequent to that time I have always been interested
by these great tangles. Seeing them as in New York
facing river banks where ships await their cargoes, or
surrounded by the tall coal pockets and grain elevators
of a crowded commercial section, I have often thought
how typical of the shift and change of life they are, how
peculiarly of this day and no other. Imagine a Roman, a
Greek, an Egyptian or an Assyrian being shown one of
these immense freight yards with their confusing mass of
cars, their engines, bells, spirals of smoke and steam, their
interesting variety of color, form and movement. How
impossible to explain to such an one the mechanism if
not the meaning of it all. How impossible it would be
for him to identify what he saw with anything that he
knew. The mysterious engines, the tireless switching,
the lights, the bells, the vehicles, the trainmen and
officials. And as far as some future age that yet may
be is concerned, all that one sees here or that relates to
this form of transportation may even in the course of a

few hundred years have vanished as completely as have
the old caravanseries of the Orient—rails, cars, engines,
coal and smoke and steam, even the intricate processes by
which present freight exchange is effected. And something entirely different may have come in its place,
transportation by air, for instance, the very mechanism
of flight and carriage directed by wireless from given
centers.

And yet, as far as life itself is concerned, its strife
and change, how typical of it are these present great
yards with their unending evidences of movement and
change. These cars that come and go, how heavy now
with freight, or import; how empty now of anything
suggesting service or use even, standing like idle, un-
needed persons upon some desolate track, while the
thunder of life and exchange passes far to one side. And
anon, as in life, each and every one of them finds itself in
the very thick of life, thundering along iron rails from
city to city, themselves, or rather their contents, eagerly
awaited and welcomed and sought after, and again left,
as before. And then the old cars, battered and sway-
backed by time and the elements and long service, standing here and there unused and useless, their chassis bent
and sometimes cracked by undue strain or rust, their
sides bulging, their roofs and doors decayed and warped
or broken, quite ready for that limbo of old cars, the
junk yard rather than the repair shop.

And yet they have been so useful, have seen and
done so much, been in such varied and interesting places
—the cities, the towns, the country stations, the lone
sidings where they have waited or rolled in sun and

rain. Here in this particular New York yard over which I am now brooding, upon a great viaduct which commands it all, is one old car, recently emptied of its load of grain, about which on this winter's day a flock of colorful pigeons are rising and falling, odd companions for such a lumbering and cumbersome thing, yet so friendly to and companionable with it, some of them walking peacefully upon its roof, others picking up remaining grains within its open door, others on the snowy ground before it picking still other fallen grains, and not at all disturbed by the puffing engines elsewhere. It might as well be a great boat accompanied by a cloud of gulls. And that other car there, that dusty, yellow one, labeled Central of Georgia, yet from which now a great wagonful of Christmas trees is being taken from Georgia, or where? Has it been to Maine or Labrabor or the Canadian north for these, and where will it go, from here, and how soon? Leaning upon this great viaduct that crosses this maze of tracks and commands so many of them, a great and interesting spectacle, I am curious as to the history or the lives of these cars, each and every one, the character of the places and lives among which each and every one of them has passed its days. They appear so wooden, so lumpish, so inert and cumbersome and yet the places they have been, the things they have seen!

I am told by the physicists that each and every atom of all of this wealth of timber and steel before me is as alive as life; that it consists, each and every particle, of a central spicule of positive energy about which revolve at great speed lesser spicules of negative energy.

And so these same continue to revolve until each particular atom, for some chemic or electronic reason, shall have been dissolved, when forthwith these spicules rearrange themselves into new forms, to revolve as industriously and as unceasingly as before. Springs the thought then: Is anything inert, lacking in response, perception, mood? And if not, what may each of these individual cars with their wealth of experience and observation think of this life, their place in it, their journeys and their strange and equally restless and unknowing companion, man?

THE FLIGHT OF PIGEONS

In all the city there is no more beautiful sight than that which is contributed by the flight of pigeons. You may see them flying in one place and another, here over the towering stacks of some tall factory, there over the low roofs of some workaday neighborhood; the yard of a laborer, the roof of some immense office building, the eaves of a shed or barn furnishing them shelter and a point of rendezvous from which they sail. I have seen them at morning, when the sky was like silver, turning in joyous circles so high that the size of a large flock of forty was no more than a hand's breadth. I have seen them again at evening, wheeling and turning in a light which was amethystine in its texture, so soft that they seemed swimming in a world of dream. In the glow of a radiant sunset, against the bosom of lowering storm clouds, when the turn of a wing made them look like a handful of snowflakes, or the shafts of the evening sunlight turned their bodies to gold, I have watched them soaring, soaring, soaring, running like children, laughing down the bosom of the wind, wheeling, shifting, rising, falling, the one idyllic note in a world of commonplace—or, perhaps more truthfully, the key central of what is a heavenly scene of beauty.

I do not know what it is that makes pigeons so interesting to me, unless it is that this flight of theirs into the upper world is to me the essence of things poetic, the one thing which I should like to do myself. The sunny sides of the barnyard roofs they occupy, the quiet beauty of the yards in which they live, their graceful and contented acceptance of the simple and the commonplace, their cooing ease, the charm of the landscapes over which they fly and against the outlines of which they are so often artistically engraved, are to me of the essence of the beautiful. I can think of nothing better. If I were to have the privilege of reincarnation I might even choose to be a pigeon.

And, in connection with this, I have so often asked myself what there is in pure motion which is so delightful, so enchanting, and before the mystery of which, as manifested by the flight of pigeons my mind pauses, for it finds no ready solution. The poetry of music, the poetry of motion, the arch-significance of a graceful line in flight—these are of psychic, perhaps of chemic subtlety (who knows?), blending into some great scheme of universal rhythm, of which singing, dancing, running, flying, the sinuous curvings of rivers, the rhythmic wavings of trees, the blowings and restings of the winds, and every other lovely thing of which the earth is heir, are but integral parts.

Nature has many secrets all her own. We peer and search. With her ill moods we quarrel. Over her savageries we weep or rage. In her amethystine hours of ease and rest we rest also and wonder, moved to profound and regal melancholy over our own brief hours in her light, to unreasoned joy and laughter over her beauty in her better moods, their pensive exaltation.

As for myself, I only know that whenever I see these birds, their coats of fused slate and bright metallic colors shielding them so smoothly, their feet of coral, their eyes of liquid black, smooth-rimmed with pink, and strutting so soberly at ease on every barn roof or walk or turning, awing, in some heavenly light against a sky of blue or storm-black—I only know that once more a fugue of most delicate and airy mood is being fingered, that the rendition of another song is at hand.

To fly so! To be a part of sky, sunlight, air! To be thus so delicately and gracefully organized as to be able to rest upon the bosom of a breeze, or run down its curving surface in long flights, to have the whole world-side for a spectacle, the sunny roof of a barn or a house for a home! Not to brood over the immensities, perhaps, not to sigh over the too-well-known end!

Fold you your hands and gaze. . . . They speak of joy accomplished. Fold your hands and gaze. As you look you have that which they bring—beauty. It is without flaw and without price.

ON BEING POOR

POVERTY is so relative. I have lived to be thirty-two now, and am just beginning to find that out. Hitherto, in no vague way, poverty to me seemed to be indivisibly united with the lack of money. And this in the face of a long series of experiences which should have proved to any sane person that this was only relatively true. Without money, or at times with so little that an ordinary day laborer would have scoffed at my supply, I still found myself meditating gloomily and with much show of reason upon the poverty of others. But what I was really complaining of, if I had only known, was not poverty of material equipment (many of those whom I pitied were materially as well if not better supplied than I was) but poverty of mind, the most dreadful and inhibiting and destroying of all forms of poverty. There are others, of course: Poverty of strength, of courage, of skill. And in respect to no one of these have I been rich, but poverty of mind, of the understanding, of taste, of imagination—therein lies the true misery, the freezing degradation of life.

For I walk through the streets of this great city—so many of them no better than the one in which I live— and see thousands upon thousands, materially no worse

off than myself, many of them much better placed, yet
with whom I would not change places save under conditions that could not be met, the principal one being that
I be permitted to keep my own mind, my own point of
view. For here comes one whose clothes are good but
tasteless, or dirty; and I would not have his taste or his
dirt. And here is another whose shabby quarters cost him
as much as do mine and more, and yet I would not live in
the region which he chooses for half his rent, nor have
his mistaken notion of what is order, beauty, comfort.
Nothing short of force could compel me. And here is one
sufficiently well dressed and housed, as well dressed and
housed as myself, who still consorts with friends from
whom I could take no comfort, creatures of so poor a
mentality that it would be torture to associate with them.

And yet how truly poor, materially, I really am.
For over a year now the chamber in which I dwell has
cost me no more than four dollars a week. My clothes,
with the exception of such minor changes as ties and
linen, are the very same I have had for several years. I
am so poor at this writing that I have not patronized a
theater in months. A tasteful restaurant such as always
I would prefer has this long while been beyond my
purse. I have even been beset by a nervous depression
which has all but destroyed my power to write, or to
sell that which I might write. And, as I well know,
illness and death might at any time interefere and cut
short the struggle that in my case has thus far proved
materially most profitless; and yet, believe me, I have
never felt poor, or that I have been cheated of much

that life might give. Nor have I felt that sense of poverty that appears to afflict thousands of those about me.

I cannot go to a theater, for instance, lacking the means. But I can and do go to many of the many, many museums, exhibits, collections and arboreta that are open to me for nothing in this great city. And for greater recreation even, I turn to such books of travel, of discovery, of scientific and philosophic investigation and speculation as chance to fit in with my mood at the time and with which a widespread public beneficence has provided me, and where I find such pleasure, such relief, such delight as I should hesitate to attempt to express in words.

But apart from these, which are after all but reports of and commentaries upon the other, comes the beauty, of life itself. I know it to be a shifting, lovely, changeful thing ever, and to it, the spectacle of it as a whole, in my hours of confusion and uncertainty I invariably return, and find such marvels of charm in color, tone, movement, arrangement, which, had I the genius to report, would fill the museums and the libraries of the world to overflowing with its masterpieces. The furies of snow and rain that speed athwart a hidden sun. The wracks and wisps of cloud that drape a winter or a summer moon. A distant, graceful tower from which a flock of pigeons soar. The tortuous, tideful rivers that twist among great forests of masts and under many graceful bridges. The crowding, surging ways of seeking men. These cost me nothing, and I weary of them never.

And sunsets. And sunrises. And moonsets. And moonrises. These are not things to which those materially deficient would in the main turn for solace, but to me they are substances of solace, the major portion of all my wealth or possible wealth, in exchange for which I would not take a miser's hoard. I truly would not.

SIX O'CLOCK

THE hours in which the world is working are numerous and always fascinating. It is not the night-time or the Sabbath or the day of pleasure that counts, but the day's work. Whether it be as statesman or soldier, poet or laborer, the day's work is the thing. And at the end of the day's work, in its commoner forms at least, comes the signal of its accomplishment, the whistle, the bell, the fading light, the arresting face of the clock.

To me, personally, there is no hour which quite equals that which heralds the close of the day's toil. I know, too, that others are important, the getting up and lying down of men, but this of ceasing after a day's work, when we lay down the ax or the saw, or the pen or pencil, stay our machine, take off our apron and quit—that is wonderful. Others may quit earlier. The lawyer and the merchant and the banker may cease their labors an hour earlier. The highly valued clerk or official is not opposed if he leaves at four-thirty or at five, and at five-thirty skilled labor generally may cease. But at six o'clock the rank and file are through, "the great unwashed," as they have been derisively termed, the real laboring man and laboring woman. It is for them then that the six o'clock whistle blows; that the six o'clock bell strikes; it is for them that the evening lamps are lit in millions of homes; it is for them that the blue smoke of

81

an evening fire curls upward at nightfall and that the street cars and vehicles of transfer run thick and black.

The streets are pouring with them at six o'clock. They are as a great tide in the gray and dark. They come bearing their baskets and buckets, their armfuls of garnered wood, their implements of labor and of accomplishment, and their faces streaked with the dirt of their toil. While you and I, my dear sir, have been sitting at our ease this last hour they have been working, and where we began at nine they began at seven. They have worked all day, not from seven-thirty until five-thirty or from nine until four, but from seven to six, and they are weary.

You can see it in their faces. Some have a lean, pinched appearance as though they were but poorly nourished or greatly enervated. Some have a furtive, hurried look, as though the problem of rent and food and clothing were inexplicable and they were thinking about it all the time. Some are young yet and unscathed —the most are young (for the work of the world is done by the youth of the world)—and they do not see as yet to what their labor tends. Nearly all are still lightened with a sense of opportunity; for what may the world not hold in store? Are not its bells still tinkling, its lights twinkling? Are not youth and health and love the solvents of all our woes?

These crowds when the whistles blow come as great movements of the sea come. If you stand in the highways of traffic they are at once full to overflowing. If you watch the entrance to great mills they pour forth a living stream, dark, energetic, undulant. To see them melting away into the highways and byways is like seeing a stream tumble and sparkle, like listening to the fading echoes of a great bell. They come, vivid, vibrant, like a deep, full-throated note. They go again as bell notes finally go.

If you stand at the entrance of one of our great industrial institutions you may see for yourself. Its walls are like those of a prison, tall, dark, many-windowed; its sound like that of a vast current of water pouring over a precipice. Inside a thousand or a hundred thousand shuttles may be crashing; I know not. Patient figures are hurrying to and fro. You may see them through the brightly lighted windows of a winter's night. Suddenly the great whistle sounds somewhere in the thick of the city. Then another and another. In a moment a score and a hundred siren voices are calling out the hour of cessation and the rush of the great world of machinery is stilling. The figures disappear from the machines. The tiny doors at the bottom of the walls open. Out they come, hurrying, white-faced, black-shawled, the vast contingent of men and boys, girls and children; into the black night they hurry, the fresh winds sweeping about their insignificant figures. This is but one mill and all over the world as the planet rolls eastward these whistles are blowing, the factories are ceasing, the figures are pouring forth.

It is on such as these, O students of economics, that all our fine-spun fancies of life are based. It is on such as these that our statecraft is erected. Kings sit in palaces, statesmen confer in noble halls, because of these and such as these. The science of government

—it *is* because of these. The art of production—it is by and for these. The importance of distribution—it concerns these. All our carefully woven theories of morals, of health, of property—they have these for their being; without them they are not.

The world runs with a rushing tide of life these days. It has broken forth into a veritable storm of creation. Men are born by the millions. They die in great masses silently. To-day they are here, to-morrow cut down and put away. But in these crowds of workers we see the flower of it all, the youth, the enthusiasm, the color. Life is here at its highest, not death. There are no sick here: they have dropped out. There are no halt, or very few, no lame. All the weaklings have been cut down and there remains here, running in a hurrying, sparkling stream, the energy, the strength, the hope of the world. That they may not be too hardly used is obvious, for then life itself ceases; that they may not be too utterly brutalized is sure, for then life itself becomes too brutal for endurance. That they may only be driven in part is a material truism. They cannot be driven too far; they must be led in part. For that the maxim, "Feed my sheep."

But in the spectacle of living there is none other like this. It is all that life may ever be, energetic, hungry, eager. It is the hope of the world, and the yearning of the world concentrated. Here are passion, desire, despair, running eagerly away. The great whistles of the world sound their presence nightly. The sinking of the sun marks their sure approach. It is six o'clock, and the work of the day is ended—for the night.

THE TOILERS OF THE TENEMENTS

NEW YORK CITY has one hundred thousand people who, under unfavorable conditions, work with their fingers for so little money that they are understood, even by the uninitiated general public, to form a class by themselves. These are by some called sewing-machine workers, by others tenement toilers, and by still others sweatshop employees; but, in a general sense, the term, tenement workers, includes them all. They form a great section in one place, and in others little patches, ministered to by storekeepers and trade agents who are as much underpaid and nearly as hard-working as they themselves.

Go into any one of these areas and you will encounter a civilization that is as strange and un-American as if it were not included in this land at all. Pushcarts and market-stalls are among the most distinctive features. Little stores and grimy windows are also characteristic of these sections. There is an atmosphere of crowdedness and poverty which goes with both. Any one can see that these people are living energetically. There is something about the hurry and enthusiasm of their life that reminds you of ants.

If you stay and turn your attention from the traffic proper, the houses begin to attract your attention. They are nearly all four-story or five-story buildings, with here and there one of six, and still another of seven stories; all without elevators, and all, with the exception of the last,

exceedingly old. There are narrow entrance-ways, dingy
and unlighted, which lead up dark and often rickety
stairs. There are other alley-ways, which lead, like narrow tunnels, to rear tenements and back shops. Iron fire
escapes descend from the roof to the first floor, in every
instance, because the law compels it. Iron stairways
sometimes ascend, where no other means of entrance is to
be had. There are old pipes which lead upward and
carry water. No such thing as sanitary plumbing exists.
You will not often see a gas-light in a hall in as many as
two blocks of houses. You will not see one flat in ten
with hot and cold water arrangements. Other districts
have refrigerators and stationary washstands, and bath
tubs as a matter of course, but these people do not know
what modern conveniences mean. Steam heat and hot
and cold water tubs and sinks have never been installed
in this area.

The houses are nearly all painted a dull red, and nearly
all are divided in the most unsanitary manner. Originally they were built five rooms deep, with two flats on a
floor, but now the single flats have been subdivided and
two or three, occasionaly four or five, families live and
toil in the space which was originally intended for one.
There are families so poor, or so saving and unclean, that
they huddle with other families, seven or eight persons
in two rooms. Iron stands covered by plain boards
make a bed which can be enlarged or reduced at will.
When night comes, four, five, six, sometimes seven such
people stretch out on these beds. When morning comes
the bedclothes, if such they may be called, are cleared
away and the board basis is used as a table. One room

holds the stove, the cooking utensils, the chairs, and the sewing machine. The other contains the bed, the bed-clothing, and various kinds of stored material. Eating, sleeping, and usually some washing are done there.

I am giving the extreme instances, unfortunately common to the point of being numerous. In the better instances three or four people are housed in two rooms. How many families there are that live less closely quartered than this would not be very easy to say. On the average, five people live in two rooms. A peddler or a pushcart man who can get to where he can occupy two rooms, by having his wife and children work, is certain that he is doing well. Fathers and mothers, sons and daughters, go out to work. If the father cannot get work and the mother can, then that is the order of procedure. If the daughter cannot get work and the mother and father can, it is the daughter's duty to take care of the house and take in sewing. If any of the boys and girls are too young to go out and enter the shops, duty compels them to help on the piecework that is taken into the rooms. Everything is work, in one form or another, from morning until night.

As for the people themselves, they are a strange mixture of all races and all creeds. Day after day you will see express wagons and trucks leaving the immigration station at the Battery, loaded to crowding with the latest arrivals, who are being taken as residents to one or another colony of this crowded section. There are Greeks, Italians, Russians, Poles, Syrians, Armenians and Hungarians. Jews are so numerous that they have to be classified with the various nations whose language they speak. All are poverty-stricken, all venturing into this new world to make their living. The vast majority have absolutely nothing more than the ten dollars which the immigration inspectors are compelled to see that they have when they arrive. These people recruit the territory in question.

In the same hundred thousand, and under the same tenement conditions, are many who are not foreign-born. I know personally of American fathers who have got down to where it is necessary to work as these foreigners work. There are home-grown American mothers who have never been able to lift themselves above the conditions in which they find themselves to-day. Thousands of children born and reared in New York City are growing up under conditions which would better become a slum section of Constantinople.

I know a chamber in this section where, at a plain wooden bench or table, sits a middle-aged Hungarian and his wife, with a fifteen-year-old daughter, sewing. The Hungarian is perhaps not honestly Gentile, for he looks as if he might have Hebrew blood in his veins. The mother and the daughter partake of a dark olive tinge, more characteristic of the Italian than of anything else. It must be a coincidence, however, for these races rarely mix. Between them and upon a nearby chair are piled many pairs of trousers, all awaiting their labor. Two buckles and a button must be sewed on every one. The rough edges at the bottom must be turned up and basted,

and the inside about the top must be lined with a kind
of striped cotton which is already set loosely in place.
It is their duty to sew closely with their hands what is
already basted. No machine worker can do this work,
and so it is sent out to such as these, under the practice
of tenement distribution. Their duty is to finish it.

There would be no need to call attention to these
people except that in this instance they have unwittingly
violated the law. Tenement workers, under the new
dispensation, cannot do exactly as they please. It is
not sufficient for them to have an innate and necessitous
desire to work. They must work under special conditions. Thus, it is now written that the floors must be
clean and the ceilings whitewashed. There must not be
any dirt on the walls. No room in which they work must
have such a thing as a bed in it, and no three people may
ever work together in one room. Law and order pre-
scribe that one is sufficient. These others—father and
daughter, or mother and daughter, or mother and father
—should go out into the shops, leaving just one here to
work. Such is the law.

These three people, who have only these two trades,
have complied with scarcely any of these provisions. The
room is not exactly as clean as it should be. The floor
is dirty. Overhead is a smoky ceiling, and in one corner
is a bed. The two small windows before which they labor
do not give sufficient ventilation, and so the air in the
chamber is stale. Worst of all, they are working three
in a chamber, and have no license.

"How now," asks an inspector, opening the door—
for there is very little civility of manner observed by

these agents of the law who constantly regulate these people—"any pants being finished here?"

"How?" says the Hungarian, looking purblindly up. It is nothing new to him to have his privacy thus invaded. Unless he has been forewarned and has his door locked, police and detectives, to say nothing of health inspectors and other officials, will frequently stick their heads in or walk in and inquire after one thing or another. Sometimes they go leisurely through his belongings and threaten him for concealing something. There is a general tendency to lord it over and browbeat him, for what reason he has no conception. Other officials do it in the old country; perhaps it is the rule here.

"So," says the inspector, stepping authoritatively forward, "finishing pants, eh? All three of you? Got a license?"

"Vot?" inquires the pale Hungarian, ceasing his labor.

"Where is your license—your paper? Haven't you got a paper?"

The Hungarian, who has not been in this form of work long enough to know the rules, puts his elbows on the table and gazes nervously into the newcomer's face. What is this now that the gentleman wants? His wife looks her own inquiry and speaks of it to her daughter.

"What is it he wants?" says the father to the child.

"It is a paper," returns the daughter in Hungarian. "He says we must have a license."

"Paper?" repeats the Hungarian, looking up and shaking his head in the negative. "No."

"Oh, so you haven't got a license then? I thought so. Who are you working for?"

The father stares at the child. Seeing that he does not understand, the inspector goes on: "The boss, the boss! What boss gave you these pants to finish?"

"Oh," returns the little girl, who understands somewhat better than the rest, "the boss, yes. He wants to know what boss gave us these pants." This last in a foreign tongue to her father.

"Tell him," says the mother in Hungarian, "that the name is Strakow."

"Strakow," repeats the daughter.

"Strakow, eh?" says the inspector. "Well, I'll see Mr. Strakow. You must not work on these any more. Do you hear? Listen, you," and he turns the little girl's face up to him, "you tell your father that he can't do any more of this work until he gets a license. He must go up to No. 1 Madison Avenue and get a paper. I don't know whether they'll give it to him or not, but he can go and ask. Then he must clean this floor. The ceiling must be whitewashed—see?"

The little girl nods her head.

"You can't keep this bed in here, either," he adds. "You must move the bed out into the other room if you can. You mustn't work here. Only one can work here. Two of you must go out into the shop."

All the time the careworn parents are leaning forward eagerly, trying to catch the drift of what they cannot possibly understand. Both interrupt now and then with a "What is it?" in Hungarian, which the daughter has no time to heed. She is so busy trying to understand half of it herself that there is no time for explanation. Finally she says to her parents:

"He says we cannot all work here."

"Vot?" says the father. "No vork?"

"No," replies the daughter. "Three of us can't work in one room. It's against the law. Only one. He says that only one can work in this room."

"How!" he exclaims, as the little girl goes on making vaguely apparent what these orders are. As she proceeds the old fellow's face changes. His wife leans forward, her whole attitude expressive of keen, sympathetic anxiety.

"No vork?" he repeats. "I do no more vork?"

"No," insists the inspector, "not with three in one room."

The Hungarian puts out his right leg, and it becomes apparent that an injury has befallen him. Words he pours upon his daughter, who explains that he has been a pushcart peddler but has received a severe injury to his leg and cannot walk. Helping to sew is all that he can do.

"Well," says the inspector when he hears of this, "that's too bad, but I can't help it. It's the law. You'll have to see the department about it. I can't help it."

Astonished and distressed, the daughter explains, and then they sit in silence. Five cents a pair is all they have been able to earn since the time the father became expert, and all they can do, working from five in the morning until eleven at night, is two dozen pairs a day —in other words, to earn seven dollars and twenty cents a week. If they delay for anything, as they often must.

the income drops to six, and quite often to five, dollars. Two dollars a week is their tax for rent.

"So!" says the father, his mouth open. He is too deeply stricken and nonplussed to know what to do. The mother nervously turns her hands.

"You hear now," says the inspector, taking out a tag and fastening it upon the goods—"no more work. Go and see the department."

"How?" asks the father, staring at his helpless family after the door has closed.

How indeed!

In the same round the inspector will come a little later to the shop from which the old Hungarian secured the trousers for finishing. He is armed with full authority over all of these places. In his pocket lie the tags, one of which he puts on a lot of clothing just ordered halted. If that tag is removed it is a penal offense. If it stays on no one can touch the goods until the contractor explains to the factory inspector how he has come to be giving garments for finishing to dwellers in tenements who have not a license. This is a criminal offense on his part. Now he must not touch the clothes he sent over there. If the old Hungarian returns them he must not accept them or pay him any money. This contractor and his clients offer a study in themselves.

His shop is on the third floor of a rear building, which was once used for dwelling purposes but is now given over entirely to clothing manufactories or sweatshops. A flight of dark, ill-odored, rickety stairs gives access to it. There is noise and chatter audible, a thick mixture of sounds from whirring sewing machines and muttering human beings. When you open the door a gray-haired Hebrew, whose long beard rests patriarchally upon his bosom, looks over his shoulders at you from a brick furnace, where he is picking up a reheated iron. Others glance up from their bent positions over machines and ironing-boards. It is a shadowy, hot-odored, floor-littered room.

"Have you a finisher doing work for you by the name of Koslovsky?" inquires the inspector of a thin, bright-eyed Syrian Jew, who is evidently the proprietor of this establishment.

"Koslovsky?" he says after him, in a nervous, fawning, conciliatory manner. "Koslovsky? What is he? No."

"Finisher, I said."

"Yes, finisher—finisher, that's it. He does no work for me—only a little—a pair of pants now and then."

"You knew that he didn't have a license, didn't you?"

"No, no. I did not. No license? Did he not have a license?"

"You're supposed to know that. I've told you that before. You'll have to answer at the office for this. I've tagged his goods. Don't you receive them now. Do you hear?"

"Yes," says the proprietor excitedly. "I would not receive them. He will get no more work from me. When did you do that?"

"Just this morning. Your goods will go up to headquarters."

"So," he replied weakly. "That is right. It is just so. Come over here."

The inspector follows him to a desk in the corner.

"Could you not help me out of this?" he asks, using a queer Jewish accent. "I did not know this once. You are a nice man. Here is a present for you. It is funny I make this mistake."

"No," returns the inspector, shaking his head. "Keep your money. I can't do anything. These goods are tagged. You must learn not to give out finishing to people without a license."

"That is right," he exclaims. "You are a nice man, anyhow. Keep the money."

"Why should I keep the money? You'll have to explain anyhow. I can't do anything for you."

"That is all right," persists the other. "Keep it, anyhow. Don't bother me in the future. There!"

"No, we can't do that. Money won't help you. Just observe the law—that's all I want."

"The law, the law," repeats the other curiously. "That is right. I will observe him."

Such is one story—almost the whole story. This employer, so nervous in his wrongdoings, so anxious to bribe, is but a little better off than those who work for him.

In other tenements and rear buildings are other shops and factories, but they all come under the same general description. Men, women and children are daily making coats, vests, knee-pants and trousers. There are side branches of overalls, cloaks, hats, caps, suspenders, jerseys and blouses. Some make dresses and waists, underwear and neckwear, waist bands, skirts, shirts and purses; still others, fur, or fur trimmings, feathers and artificial flowers, umbrellas, and even collars. It is all a great allied labor of needlework, needlework done by machine and finishing work done by hand. The hundred thousand that follow it are only those who are actually employed as supporters. All those who are supported—the infants, school children, aged parents, and physically disabled relatives—are left out. You may go throughout New York and Brooklyn, and wherever you find a neighborhood poor enough you will find these workers. They occupy the very worst of tumbledown dwellings. Shrewd Italians, and others called padrones, sometimes lease whole blocks from such men as William Waldorf Astor, and divide up each natural apartment into two or three. Then these cubbyholes are leased to the toilers, and the tenement crowding begins.

You will see by peculiar evidences that things have been pretty bad with these tenements in the past. For instance, between every front and back room you will find a small window, and between every back room and the hall, another. The construction of these was compelled by law, because the cutting up of a single apartment into two or three involved the sealing up of the connecting door and the shutting off of natural circulation. Hence the state decided that a window opening into the hall would be some improvement, anyhow, and so this window-cutting began. It has proved of no value, however. Nearly every such window is most certainly sealed up by the tenants themselves.

In regard to some other matters, this cold enforcement of the present law is, in most cases, a blessing, oppressive as it seems at times. Men should not crowd and stifle and die in chambers where seven occupy the natural space of one. Landlords should not compel them to, and poverty ought to be stopped from driving them. Unless the law says that the floor must be clean and the ceiling white, the occupants will never find time to make them so. Unless the beds are removed from the work-room and only one person allowed to work in one room, the struggling "sweater" will never have less than five or six suffering with him. Enforce such a law, and these workers, if they cannot work unless they comply with these conditions, will comply with them, and charge more for their labor, of course. Sweatshop manufacturers cannot get even these to work for nothing, and landlords cannot get tenants to rent their rooms unless they are clean enough for the law to allow them to work in them. Hence the burden falls in a small measure on the land-lord, but not always.

The employer or boss of a little shop, who is so nervous in wrongdoing, so anxious to bribe, is but a helpless agent in the hands of a greater boss. He is no foul oppressor of his fellow man. The great clothing con-cerns in Broadway and elsewhere are his superiors. What they give, he pays, barring a small profit to him-self. If these people are compelled by law to work less or under more expensive conditions, they must receive more or starve, and the great manufactories cannot let them actually starve. They come as near to it now as ever, but they will pay what is absolutely essential to keep them alive; hence we see the value of the law.

To grow and succeed here, though, is something very different. Working, as these people do, they have very little time for education. The great struggle is for bread, and unless the families are closely watched, children are constantly sent to work before they are twelve. I was present in one necktie factory once where five of its employees were ordered out for being without proof that they were fourteen years of age. I have personally seen shops, up to a dozen, inspected in one morning, and some struggling little underling ordered out from each.

"For why you come home?" is the puzzled inquiry of the parents at night.

"Da police maka me."

Down here, and all through this peculiar world, the police are everything. They regulate the conduct, adjudicate the quarrels, interfere with the evil-doers. The terror of them keeps many a child studying in the school-room where otherwise it would be toiling in the chamber at home or the shop outside. Still the struggle is against them, and most of them grow up without any of those advantages so common to others.

At the same time, there are many institutions established to reach these people. One sees Hebrew and Legal Aid Societies in large and imposing buildings. Outdoor recreation leagues, city playgrounds, schools, and university settlements—all are here; and yet the percentage of opportunity is not large. Parents have to struggle too hard. Their ignorant influence upon the lives of the young ones is too great.

I know a lawyer, though, of considerable local prestige, who has worked his way out of these conditions; and Broadway from Thirty-fourth Street south, to say nothing of many other streets, is lined with the signs of those who have overcome the money difficulty of lives begun under these conditions. Unfortunately the money problem, once solved, is not the only thing in the world. Their lives, although they reach to the place where they have gold signs, automobiles and considerable private pleasures, are none the more beautiful. Too often, because of these early conditions, they remain warped, oppressive, greedy and distorted in every worthy mental sense by the great fight they have made to get their money.

Nearly the only ideal that is set before these strugglers still toiling in the area, is the one of getting money. A hundred thousand children, the sons and daughters of working parents whose lives are as difficult as that of the Hungarian portrayed and whose homes are as unlovely, are inoculated in infancy with the doctrine that wealth is all,—the shabbiest and most degrading doctrine that can be impressed upon anyone.

THE END OF A VACATION

IT was the close of summer. The great mountain and lake areas to the north of New York were pouring down their thousands into the hot, sun-parched city. Vast throngs were coming back on the steamboats of the Hudson. Vaster throngs were crowding the hourly trains which whirled and thundered past the long lane of villages which stretches between Albany and New York City. The great station at Albany was packed with a perspiring mass. The several fast expresses running without stop to New York City were overwhelmed. Particularly was the Empire State Express full. In the one leaving Albany at eight in the evening passengers were standing in the aisles.

It was a little, dark, wolf of a man who fought his way and that of his wife behind him to the car steps, and out of the scrambling, pushing throng rescued a car seat. He put his back against those who were behind and stood still until his wife could crowd in. Then he took his place beside her and looked grimly around. For her part, she arranged herself indifferently and looked wearily out of the window. She was dark, piquant, petite, attractive.

Behind these two there came another person, who seemed not so anxious for a seat. While others were pushing eagerly he stepped to one side, holding his place close to the little wolf man yet looking indifferently

about him. He was young, ruddy, stalwart, an artist's
ideal of what a summer youth ought to be. And now
and then he looked in the direction of the wolf man's
wife. But there appeared to be nothing of common
understanding between them.

The train pulled out with a slow clacking sound. It
gained in headway, and lights of yard engines and those
of other cars, as well as street lamps and houses, flashed
into view and out again. Then came the long darkness
of the open country and the river bank, and the people
settled to endure the several hours in such comfort as
they could. Some read newspapers, some books. The
majority stared wearily out of the window, not attempting to talk. They were tired. The joys of their vaca-
tions were behind them. Why talk, with New York and
early work ahead?

In the midst of these stood the young athlete, rumi-
nating. In his seat before him sat the wolf man, studying a notebook. Beside him, the young wife, dark,
piquant, nervously restless, kept her face to the window,
arranging her back hair now and then with a jeweled
hand, and occasionally turning her face inward to look
at the car. It was as if a vast gulf lay between her
and her spouse, as if they were miles and miles apart,
and yet they were obviously married. You could see
that by the curt, gruff questions he addressed to her,
by the quick, laconic, uninterpretative replies. She was
weary and so was he.

The train neared Poughkeepsie. For the twentieth
or more time the jeweled hand had felt the back of her
dark piled-up hair. For the fourth or fifth time the

elbow had rested on the back of the seat, the hand falling lazily toward her cheek. Just once it dropped full length along the back ridge, safely above and beyond her husband's head and toward the hand of the standing athlete, who appeared totally unconscious of the gesture. Then it was withdrawn. A stir of interest seemed to go with it, a quick glance. There was something missing, The athlete was not looking.

At Yonkers the crowd was already beginning to stir and pull itself together. At Highbridge it was dragging satchels from the bundle racks and from beneath the seats. The little wolf man was closing up his notebook, looking darkly around. For the thirtieth time the jeweled hand felt of the dark hair, the elbow rested on the seat-top, and then for the second time the arm slipped out and rested full length, the hand touching an elbow which was now resting wearily, holding the shoulder and supporting the chin of the man who was standing. There was the throb as of an electric contact. The elbow rose ever so slightly and pressed the fingers. The eyes of the wolf's wife met the eyes of her summer ideal, and there stood revealed a whole summer romance, bright sun-shades, lovely flowers, green grass, trysting-places, a dark, dangerous romance, with a grim, unsuspecting wolf in the background. The arm was withdrawn, the hair touched, the window turned to wearily. All was over.

And yet you could see how it might continue, could feel that it would. In the very mood of the two was indicated ways and means. But now this summer contact was temporarily over. The train rolled into Grand Central Station. The crowd arose. There was a determined shuffle forward of the wolf man, with his wife close behind him, and both were gone. The athlete followed respectfully after. He gave the wolf man and his wife a wide berth. He followed, however, and looked and thought—backward into the summer, no doubt, and forward.

THE TRACK WALKER

IF you have nothing else to do some day when you are passing through the vast network of subway or railway tracks of any of the great railways running northward or westward or eastward out of New York, give a thought to the man who walks them for you, the man on whom your safety, in this particular place, so much depends.

He is a peculiar individual. His work is so very exceptional, so very different from your own. While you are sitting in your seat placidly wondering whether you are going to have a pleasant evening at the theater or whether the business to which you are about to attend will be as profitable as you desire, he is out on the long track over which you are speeding, calmly examining the bolts that hold the shining metals together. Neither rain nor sleet may deter him. The presence of intense heat or intense cold or dirt or dust is not permitted to interfere with his work. Day after day, at all hours and in all sorts of weather, he may be seen quietly plodding these iron highways, his wrench and sledge crossed over his shoulders, and if it be night, or in the subway, a lantern over one arm, his eyes riveted on the rails, carefully watching to see if any bolts are loose or any spikes sprung. In the subway or the New York

Central Tunnel, upward of two hundred cannon-ball flyers rush by him each day, on what might be called a four-track or ten-track bowling alley, and yet he dodges them all for perhaps as little as any laborer is paid. If he were not watchful, if he did not perform his work carefully and well, if he had a touch of malice or a feeling of vengefulness, he could wreck your train, mangle your body and send you praying and screaming to your Maker. There would be no sure way of detecting him.

Death lurks on the path he travels—subway or railway. Here, if anywhere, it may be said to be constantly lurking. What with the noise, which, in some places, like the subway and the various tunnels, is a perfect and continuous uproar, the smoke, which hangs like a thick, gloomy pall over everything, and the weak, ineffective lights which shine out on your near approach like will-o'-the-wisps, the chances of hearing and seeing the approach of any particular train are small. Side arches, or small pockets in the walls, in some places, are provided for the protection of the men, but these are not always to be reached in time when a train thunders out of the gloom. If you look sharp you may sometimes see a figure crouching in one of these as you scurry past. He is so close to the grinding wheels that the dust and soot of them are flung over him like a spray.

And yet for all this, the money that is paid these men is beggarly small. The work they do is not considered exceptionally valuable. Thirty to thirty-five cents an hour is all they are paid, and this for ten to twelve hours' work every day. That their lives are in constant

danger is not a factor in the matter. They are supposed
to work willingly for this, and they do. Only when one
is picked off, his body mangled by a passing train, is
the grimness of the sacrifice emphasized, and then only
for a moment. The space which such accidents receive
in the public prints is scarcely more than a line.

And now, what would you say of men who would
do this work for so little? What estimate would you
put on their mental capacity? Would you say that
they are worth only what they can be made to work
for? One of these men, an intelligent type of laborer,
not a drinker nor one who even smoked, attracted
my attention once by the punctuality with which he
crossed a given spot on his beat. He was a middle-
aged man, married, and had three children. Day after
day, week after week, he used to arrive at this particular
spot, his eye alert, his step quick, and when a train
approached he seemed to become aware of it as if by
instinct. When finally asked by me why he did not get
something better to do, he said: "I have no trade.
Where could I get more?"

This man was killed by a train. Sure as was his
instinct and keen his eye, he was nevertheless caught
one evening, and at the very place where he deemed
himself most sure. His head was completely obliterated,
and he had to be identified by his clothes. When he
was removed, another eager applicant was given his
place, and now he is walking the same tunnel with a
half-dozen others. If you question these men they will

all tell you the same story. They do not want to do what they are doing, but it is better than nothing.

Rough necessity, a sense of duty, and behold, we are as bricks and stones, to be put anywhere in the wall, at the bottom of the foundation in the dark, or at the top in the light. And who chooses for us?

THE REALIZATION OF AN IDEAL

Any quality to which the heart of man aspires it may attain. Would you have virtue in the world, establish it yourself. Would you have tenderness, be tender. It is only by acting in the name of that which you deem to be an ideal that its realization is brought to pass.

IN the crowded section of the lower East Side of New York, where poverty reigns most distressingly, there stands a church which is a true representative of the religion of the poor. It is an humble building, crowded in among the flats and tenements that make the homely neighborhood homelier, and sends a crude and distorted spire soaring significantly toward the sky. There is but little light inside, for that which the crowded flat-buildings about does not shut out is weakened by the dusty stained-glass windows through which it has to pass. An arched and dark-angled ceiling lends a sense of dignity to it and over it all broods the solemn atmosphere of simplicity and faith.

It is in this church (and no doubt others of a similar character elsewhere) that is constantly recurring the miracle of earthly faith. Here it is, hour after hour, that one sees entering out of the welter and the din of the streets those humble examples of the poor and ignorant, who come here out of the cares of many other states to rest a while and pray.

Near the door, between two large, gloomy pillars, there is a huge wooden cross, whereon is hung a life-size figure of the Christ. The hands and feet are pierced with the customary large forty-penny weight nails. The side is opened with an appalling gash, the forehead is crowned with the undying crown of thorns, which is driven down until the flesh is made to bleed.

Before this figure you may see kneeling, any day, not one but many specimens of those by whom the world has dealt very poorly. Their hands are rough, their faces worn and dull; on the gnarled and weary bodies are hung clothes of which you and I would be ashamed. Some carry bags, others huge bundles. With hands extended upward, their faces bearing the imprint of unquestioning faith, they look into the soft, pain-exhausted face of the Christ, imploring that aid and protection which the ordinary organization of society does not and cannot afford. It is in this church, as it seems to me, that the hour's great lesson of tenderness is given.

I call the world's attention to this picture with the assurance that this is the great, the beautiful, and the important lesson. If there be those who do not see in the body-racked figure of Christ an honest reiteration of an actual event, who cannot honestly admit that such a thing could have reasonably occurred, there is still a lesson just as impressive and just as binding as though it had. These people whom you see kneeling here and lifting up their hands present an actuality of faith which cannot be denied. This Christ, if to you and to me a myth, is to them a reality. And in so far as He is real to them He implies an ardent desire on the part of the whole human race for tenderness and mercy which it may be as well not to let go unanswered. For if Christ did not suffer, if His whole life-story was a fiction and a delusion, then all the yearning and all the faith of endless millions of men, who have lived believing and who died adoring, only furnishes proof that the race really needs such an ideal—that it must have tenderness and mercy to fly to or it could not exist.

Man is a hopeful animal. He lives by the belief that some good must accrue to him or that his life is not worth the living. It is this faith then, that in disaster or hours of all but unendurable misery causes him to turn in supplication to a higher power, and unless these prayers are in some measure answered, that faith can and will be destroyed, and life will and does become a shambles indeed. Hence, if one would balance peace against danger and death it becomes necessary for each to act as though the ideals of the world are in some sense real and that he in person is sponsor for them.

These prayers that are put up, and these supplications, if not addressed to the actual Christ, are nevertheless sent to that sum of human or eternal wisdom or sympathy as you will of which we are a part. If you believe that hope is beautiful and that mercy is a virtue, if you would have the world more lovely and its inhabitants more kind, if you would have goodness triumph and sorrow laid aside, then you must be ready to make good to such supplicants and supplications as fall to you the virtues thus pathetically appealed to. You must act in the name of tenderness. If you cannot or will not, by so much is the realization of human ideals, the possibility of living this life at all decently by any, made less.

THE PUSHCART MAN

ONE of the most appealing and interesting elements
in city life, particularly that metropolitan city life which
characterizes New York, is the pushcart man. This
curious creature of modest intellect and varying nation-
ality infests all the highways of the great city without
actually dominating any of them except a few streets
on the East Side. He is as hard-working, in the main, as
he is ubiquitous. His cart is so shabby, his stock in trade
so small. If he actually earns a reasonable wage it is
by dint of great energy and mere luck, for the officers
of the law in apparently every community find in the
presence of this person an alluring source of profit and
he is picked and grafted upon as is perhaps no other
member of the commonplace brotherhood of trade.

I like to see them trundling their two-wheeled vehicles
about the city, and I like to watch the patience and
the care with which they exercise their barely tolerated
profession of selling. You see them everywhere; vendors of fruit, vegetables, chestnuts on the East Side,
selling even dry goods, hardware, furs and groceries; and
elsewhere again the Greeks selling neckwear, flowers
and curios, the latter things at which an ordinary man
would look askance, but which the lower levels of society
somehow find useful.

I have seen them tramping in long files across Williamsburg Bridge at one, two and three o'clock in the
morning to the Wallabout Market in Brooklyn. And

I have seen them clambering over hucksters' wagons there and elsewhere searching for the choicest bits, which they hope to sell quickly. The market men have small consideration for them and will as lief strike or kick at them as to reach a bargain with them.

For one thing, I remember watching an old pushcart vendor one sweltering afternoon in summer from one o'clock in the afternoon to seven the same evening, and I was never more impressed with the qualities which make for success in this world, qualities which are rare in American life, or in any life, for that matter, for patience and good nature and sturdy charitable endurance are not common qualities anywhere.

He had his stand at Sixth Avenue and Twenty-third Street, New York, then the center of the shopping life of the city—or I had better say that he attempted to keep it there, for he was not altogether successful. He was a dark, gray-headed, grizzle-cheeked "guinea" or "dago," as he was scornfully dubbed by the Irish policeman who made his life a burden. His eye was keen, his motion quick, his general bodily make-up active, despite the fact that he was much over fifty years of age.

"That's a good one," the Irish policeman observed to me in passing, noting that I was looking at him. "He's a fox. A fine time I have keeping my eye on him."

The old Italian seemed to realize that we were talking about him for he shifted the position of his cart nervously, moving it forward a few feet. Finding himself undisturbed, he remained there. Presently, however, a heavy ice-wagon lumbered up from the west and swung in with a reckless disregard of the persons, property and privileges of the vendors who were thus unobtrusively grouped together. At the same time the young Irish-American driver raised his voice in a mighty bellow:

"Get out of there! Move on out! What the hell d'ye want to block up the street for, anyway? Go on!"

With facile manipulation of his reins he threw his wagon tongue deliberately among them and did his best to cause some damage in order to satisfy his own passing irritation.

All three vendors jumped to the task of extricating their carts, but I could not help distinguishing the oldest of the three for the dexterity with which he extricated his and the peaceful manner in which he pushed it away. The lines of his face remained practically undisturbed. All his actions denoted a remarkable usedness to difficulty. Not once did he look back, either to frown or complain. Instead, his only concern was to discover the whereabouts of the policeman. For him he searched the great crowd in every direction, even craning his neck a little. When he had satisfied himself that the coast was clear, he pushed in close to the sidewalk again and began his wait for customers.

While he was thus waiting the condition of his cart and the danger of an unobserved descent on the part of a policeman engaged his entire attention. Some few peaches had fallen awry, and these he busily straightened. One pile of those which he was selling "two for five" had now become low and this he replenished from baskets of hitherto undisturbed peaches, carefully dusting the fuzz off each one with a small brush in order to

heighten their beauty and add to the attractiveness
of the pile. Incidentally his eye was upon the crowd,
for every once in a while his arm would stretch out
in a most dramatic manner, inviting a possible pur-
chaser with his subtle glance.

"Peaches! Fine! Peaches! Fine! Fine!"

Whenever a customer came close enough, these words
were called to him in a soft, persuasive tone. He would
bend gracefully forward, pick up a peach as if the mere
lifting of it were a sufficient inducement, take up a paper
bag as if the possible transaction were an assured thing,
and look engagingly into the passerby's eyes. When it
was really settled that a purchase was intended, no word,
however brief, could fail to convey to him the import of
the situation and the number of peaches desired.

"Five—ten." The mention of a sum of money.
"These," or your hand held up, would bring quickly
what you desired.

Grace was the perfect word with which to describe
this man's actions.

From one until seven o'clock of this sweltering afternoon, every moment of his time was occupied. The
police made it difficult for him to earn his living, for
the simple reason that they were constantly making
him move on. Not only the regular policemen of the
beat, but the officers of the crossing, and the wandering
wayfarers from other precincts all came forward at
different times and hurried him away.

"Get out, now!" ordered one, in a rough and even
brutal tone. "Move on. If I catch you around here any
more to-day I'll lock you up."

The old Italian lowered his eyes and hustled his cart out into the sun.

"And don't you come back here any more," the policeman called after him; then turning to me he exclaimed: "Begob, a man pays a big license to keep a store, and these dagos come in front of his place and take all his business. They ought to be locked up —all of them."

"Haven't they a right to stand still for a moment?" I inquired.

"They have," he said, 'but they haven't any right to stand in front of any man's place when he don't want them there. They drive me crazy, keeping them out of here. I'll shoot some of them yet."

I looked about to see what if any business could be injured by their stopping and selling fruit, but found only immense establishments dealing in dry goods, drugs, furniture and the like. Some one may have complained, but it looked much more like an ordinary case of official bumptiousness or irritation.

At that time, being interested in such types, I chose to follow this one, to see what sort of a home life lay behind him. It was not difficult. By degrees, and much harried by the police, his cart with only a partially de-pleted stock was pushed to the lower East Side, in Eliza-beth Street, to be exact. Here he and his family—a wife and three or four children—occupied two dingy rooms in a typical East Side tenement. Whether he was at peace with his swarthy, bewrinkled old helpmate I do not know, but he appeared to be, and with his several partially grown children. On his return, two of them, a boy and a girl, greeted him cheerfully, and later, finding me interested and following him, and assuming that I was an officer of the law, quickly explained to me what their father did.

"He's a peddler," said the boy. "He peddles fruit."

"And where does he get his fruit?" I asked.

"Over by the Wallabout. He goes over in the morning."

I recalled seeing the long procession of vendors beating a devious way over the mile or more of steel bridge that spans the East River at Delancey Street, at one and two and three of a winter morning. Could this old man be one of these tramping over and tramping back before daylight?"

"Do you mean to say that he goes over every day?"

"Sure."

The old gentleman, by now sitting by a front window waiting for his dinner and gazing down into the sun-baked street not at all cooled by the fall of night, looked down and for some reason smiled. I presume he had seen me earlier in the afternoon. He could not know what we were talking about, however, but he sensed something. Or perhaps it was merely a feeling of the need of being pleasant.

Upon making my way to the living room and kitchen, as I did, knowing that I could offer a legal pretext, I found the same shabby and dark, but not dirty. An oil stove burned dolefully in the rear. Mrs. Pushcart Man was busy about the evening meal.

The smirks. The genuflections.

"And how much does your father make a day?" I finally asked, after some other questions.

This is a lawless question anywhere. It earned its own reward. The son inquired of the father in Italian. The latter tactfully shrugged his shoulders and held out his hands. His wife laughed and shrugged her shoulders.

" 'One, two dollars,' he says," said the boy.

There was no going back of that. He might have made more. Why should he tell anybody—the police or any one else?

And so I came away.

But the case of this one seemed to me to be so typical of the lot of many in our great cities. All of us are so pushed by ambition as well as necessity. Yet all the feelings and intuitions of the average American-born citizen are more or less at variance with so shrewd an acceptance of difficulties. We hurry more, fret and strain more, and yet on the whole pretend to greater independence. But have we it? I am sure not. When one looks at the vast army of clerks and underlings, pushing, scheming, straining at their social leashes so hopelessly and wearing out their hearts and brains in a fruitless effort to be what they cannot, one knows that they are really no better off and one wishes for them a measure of this individual's enduring patience.

A VANISHED SEASIDE RESORT

AT Broadway and Twenty-third Street, where later, on this and some other ground, the once famed Flatiron Building was placed, there stood at one time a smaller building, not more than six stories high, the northward looking blank wall of which was completely covered with a huge electric sign which read:

SWEPT BY OCEAN BREEZES
THE GREAT HOTELS
PAIN'S FIREWORKS
SOUSA'S BAND
SEIDL'S GREAT ORCHESTRA
THE RACES
NOW—MANHATTAN BEACH—NOW

Each line was done in a different color of lights, light green for the ocean breezes, white for Manhattan Beach and the great hotels, red for Pain's fireworks and the races, blue and yellow for the orchestra and band. As one line was illuminated the others were made dark, until all had been flashed separately, when they would again be flashed simultaneously and held thus for a time. Walking up or down Broadway of a hot summer night, this sign was an inspiration and an invitation. It made one long to go to Manhattan Beach. I had heard as much or more about Atlantic City and Coney Island, but this blazing sign lifted Manhattan Beach into rivalry with fairyland.

"Where is Manhattan Beach?" I asked of my brother once on my first coming to New York. "Is it very far from here?"

"Not more than fifteen miles," he replied. "That's the place you ought to see. I'll take you there on Sunday if you will stay that long."

Since I had been in the city only a day or two, and Sunday was close at hand, I agreed. When Sunday came we made our way, via horse-cars first to the East Thirty-fourth Street ferry and then by ferry and train, eventually reaching the beach about noon.

Never before, except possibly at the World's Fair in Chicago, had I ever seen anything to equal this seaward-moving throng. The day was hot and bright, and all New York seemed anxious to get away. The crowded streets and ferries and trains! Indeed, Thirty-fourth Street near the ferry was packed with people carrying bags and parasols and all but fighting each other to gain access to the dozen or more ticket windows. The boat on which we crossed was packed to suffocation, and all such ferries as led to Manhattan Beach of summer week-ends for years afterward, or until the automobile arrived, were similarly crowded. The clerk and his prettiest girl, the actress and her admirer, the actor and his playmate, brokers, small and exclusive trades-men, men of obvious political or commercial position, their wives, daughters, relatives and friends, all were outbound toward this much above the average resort.

It was some such place, I found, as Atlantic City and Asbury Park are to-day, yet considerably more restricted. There was but one way to get there, unless one could

travel by yacht or sail-boat, and that was via train service across Long Island. As for carriage roads to this
wonderful place there were none, the intervening distance being in part occupied by marsh grass and water.
The long, hot, red trains leaving Long Island City
threaded a devious way past many pretty Long Island
villages, until at last, leaving possible home sites behind,
the road took to the great meadows on trestles, and
traversing miles of bending marsh grass astir in the
wind, and crossing a half hundred winding and mucky
lagoons where lay water as agate in green frames and
where were white cranes, their long legs looking like
reeds, standing in the water or the grass, and the occasional boat of a fisherman hugging some mucky bank,
it arrived finally at the white sands of the sea and this
great scene. White sails of small yachts, the property
of those who used some of these lagoons as a safe harbor, might be seen over the distant grass, their sails
full spread, as one sped outward on these trains. It
was romance, poetry, fairyland.

And the beach, with its great hotels, held and contained all summer long all that was best and most
leisurely and pleasure-loving in New York's great middle
class of that day. There were, as I knew all the time,
other and more exclusive or worse beaches, such as
those at Newport and Coney Island, but this was one
which served a world which was plainly between the two,
a world of politicians and merchants, and dramatic and
commercial life generally. I never saw so many pros-
perous-looking people in one place, more with better and
smarter clothes, even though they were a little showy.

The straw hat with its blue or striped ribbon, the flannel suit with its accompanying white shoes, light cane, the pearl-gray derby, the check suit, the diamond and pearl pin in necktie, the silk shirt. What a cool, summery, airy-fairy realm!

And the women! I was young and not very experienced at the time, hence the effect, in part. But as I stepped out of the train at the beach that day and walked along the boardwalks which paralleled the sea, looking now at the blue waters and their distant white sails, now at the great sward of green before the hotels with its formal beds of flowers and its fountains, and now at the enormous hotels themselves, the Manhattan and the Oriental, each with its wide veranda packed with a great company seated at tables or in rockers, eating, drinking, smoking and looking outward over gardens to the blue sea beyond, I could scarcely believe my eyes—the airy, colorful, summery costumes of the women who made it, the gay, ribbony, flowery hats, the brilliant parasols, the beach swings and chairs and shades and the floating diving platforms. And the costumes of the women bathing. I had never seen a seaside bathing scene before. It seemed to me that the fabled days of the Greeks had returned. These were nymphs, nereids, sirens in truth. Old Triton might well have raised his head above the blue waves and sounded his spiral horn.

And now my brother explained to me that here in these two enormous hotels were crowded thousands who came here and lived the summer through. The wealth, as I saw it then, which permitted this! Some few Western senators and millionaires brought their yachts and private cars. Senator Platt, the State boss, along with one or more of the important politicians of the State, made the Oriental, the larger and more exclusive of the two hotels, his home for the summer. Along the verandas of these two hotels might be seen of a Saturday afternoon or of a Sunday almost the entire company of Brooklyn and New York politicians and bosses, basking in the shade and enjoying the beautiful view and the breezes. It was no trouble for any one acquainted with the city to point out nearly all of those most famous on Broadway and in the commercial and political worlds. They swarmed here. They lolled and greeted and chatted. The bows and the recognitions were innumerable. By dusk it seemed as though nearly all had nodded or spoken to each other.

And the interesting and to me different character of the amusements offered here! Out over the sea, at one end of the huge Manhattan Hotel, had been built a circular pavilion of great size, in which by turns were housed Seidl's great symphony orchestra and Sousa's band. Even now I can hear the music carried by the wind of the sea. As we strolled along the beach wall or sat upon one or the other of the great verandas we could hear the strains of either the orchestra or the band. Beyond the hotels, in a great field surrounded by a board fence, began at dusk, at which time the distant lighthouses over the bay were beginning to blink, a brilliant display of fireworks, almost as visible to the public as to those who paid a dollar to enter the grounds. Earlier in the afternoon I saw many whose only desire appeared to be to reach the race track in time for the afternoon races. There were hundreds and even thousands of others to whom the enclosed beach appeared to be all. The hundreds of dining-tables along the veranda of the Manhattan facing the sea seemed to call to still other hundreds. And yet again the walks among the parked flowers, the wide walk along the sea, and the more exclusive verandas of the Oriental, which provided no restaurant but plenty of rocking-chairs, seemed to draw still other hundreds, possibly thousands.

But the beauty of it all, the wonder, the airy, insubstantial, almost transparent quality of it all! Never before had I seen the sea, and here it was before me, a great, blue, rocking floor, its distant horizon dotted with white sails and the smoke of but faintly visible steamers dissolving in the clear air above them. Wide-winged gulls were flying by. Hardy rowers in red and yellow and green canoes paddled an uncertain course beyond the breaker line. Flowers most artfully arranged decorated the parapet of the porch, and about us rose a babel of laughing and joking voices, while from somewhere came the strains of a great orchestra, this time within one of the hotels, mingling betimes with the smash of the waves beyond the seawall. And as dusk came on, the lights of the lighthouses, and later the glimmer of the stars above the water, added an impressive and to me melancholy quality to it all. It was so insubstantial and yet so beautiful. I was so wrought up by it that I could scarcely eat. Beauty, beauty, beauty—that was the message and the import of it all, beauty that changes and fades and will not stay. And the eternal search for beauty. By the hard processes of trade, profit and loss, and the driving forces of ambition and necessity and the love of and search for pleasure, this very wonderful thing had been accomplished. Unimportant to me then, how hard some of these people looked, how selfish or vain or indifferent! By that which they sought and bought and paid for had this thing been achieved, and it was beautiful. How sweet the sea here, how beautiful the flowers and the music and these parading men and women. I saw women and girls for the favor of any one of whom, in the first flush of youthful ebullience and ignorance, I imagined I would have done anything. And at the very same time I was being seized with a tremendous depression and dissatisfaction with myself. Who was I? What did I amount to? What must one do to be worthy of all this? How little of all this had I known or would ever know! How little of true beauty or fortune or love! It mattered not that life for me was only then beginning, that I was seeing much and might yet see much more; my heart was miserable. I could have invested and beleaguered the world with my unimportant desires and my capacity. How dare life, with its brutal non-perception of values, withhold so much from one so worthy as myself and give so much to others? Why had not the dice of fortune been loaded in my favor instead of theirs? Why, why, why? I made a very doleful companion for my very good brother, I am sure.

And yet, at that very time I was asking myself who was I that I should complain so, and why was I not content to wait? Those about me, as I told myself, were better swimmers, that was all. There was nothing to be done about it. Life cared no whit for anything save strength and beauty. Let one complain as one would, only beauty or strength or both would save one. And all about, in sky and sea and sun, was that relentless force, illimitable oceans of it, which seemed not to know man, yet one tiny measure of which would make him of the elect of the earth. In the dark, over the whispering and muttering waters, and under the bright stars and in eyeshot of the lamps of the sea, I hung brooding, listening, thinking; only, after a time, to return to the hot city and the small room that was mine to meditate on what life could do for one if it would. The flowers it could strew in one's path! The beauty it could offer one—without price, as I then imagined—the pleasures with which it could beset one's path.

With what fever and fury it is that the heart seeks in youth. How intensely the little flame of life burns! And yet where is its true haven? What is it that will truly satisfy it? Has any one ever found it? In subsequent years I came by some of the things which my soul at that time so eagerly craved, the possession of which I then imagined would satisfy me, but was mine or any other heart ever really satisfied? No. And again no.

Each day the sun rises, and with it how few with whom a sense of contentment dwells! For each how many old dreams unfulfilled, old and new needs unsatisfied. Onward, onward is the lure; what life may still do, not what it has done, is the all-important. And to ask of any one that he count his blessings is but an ungrateful bit of meddling at best. He will none of it. At twenty, at thirty, at sixty, at eighty, the lure is still there, however feeble. More and ever more. Only the wearing of the body, the snapping of the string, the weakening of the inherent urge, ends the search. And with it comes the sad by-thought that what is not realized here may never again be anywhere. For if not here, where is that which could satisfy it as it is here? Of all pathetic dreams that which pictures a spiritual salvation elsewhere for one who has failed in his dreams here is the thinnest and palest, a beggar's dole indeed. But that youthful day by the sea!

*   *   *   *   *

Twenty-five years later I chanced to visit a home on the very site of one of these hotels, a home which was a part of a new real-estate division. But of that old, sweet, fair, summery life not a trace. Gone were the great hotels, the wall, the flowers, the parklike nature of the scene. In twenty-five years the beautiful circular pavilion had fallen into the sea and a part of the grounds of the great Manhattan Hotel had been eaten away by winter storms. The Jersey Coast, Connecticut, Atlantic City, aided by the automobile, had superseded and effaced all this. Even the great Oriental, hanging on for a few years and struggling to accommodate itself to new conditions, had at last been torn down. Only the beach remained, and even that was changed to meet new conditions. The land about and beyond the hotels had been filled in, planted to trees, divided by streets and sold to those who craved the freshness of this seaside isle.

But of this older place not one of those with whom I visited knew aught. They had never seen it, had but dimly heard of it. So clouds gather in the sky, are perchance illuminated by the sun, dissolve, and are gone. And youth, viewing old realms of grandeur or terror, views the world as new, untainted, virgin, a realm to be newly and freshly exploited—as, in truth, it ever is.

But we who were——!

THE BREAD-LINE

IT is such an old subject in New York. It has been here so long. For thirty-five or forty years newspapers and magazines have discussed the bread-line, and yet there it is, as healthy and vigorous a feature of the city as though it were something to be desired. And it has grown from a few applicants to many, from a small line to a large one. And now it is a sight, an institution, like a cathedral or a monument.

A curious thing, when you come to think of it. Poverty is not desirable. Its dramatic aspect may be worth something to those who are not poor, for prosperous human nature takes considerable satisfaction in proclaiming: "Lord, I am not as other men," and having it proved to itself. But this thing, from any point of view is a pathetic and a disagreeable thing, something you would feel the city as a corporation would prefer to avoid. And yet there it is.

For the benefit of those who have not seen it I will describe it again, though the task is a wearisome one and I have quite another purpose than that of description in doing so. The scene is the side door of a bakery, once located at Ninth Street and Broadway, and now moved to Tenth and Broadway, the line extending toward the west and Fifth Avenue, where formerly it was to the east and Fourth Avenue. It is composed of the usual shabby figures, men of all ages, from fifteen or younger to seventy. The line is not allowed to form before eleven o'clock, and at this hour perhaps a single figure will shamble around the corner and halt on the edge of the sidewalk. Then others, for though they appear to come slowly, some dubiously, they almost all arrive one at a time. Haste is seldom manifest in their approach. Figures appear from every direction, limping slowly, slouching stupidly, or standing with assumed or real indifference, until the end of the line is reached, when they take their places and wait.

A low murmur of conversation begins after a time, but for the most part the men stand in stupid, unbroken silence. Here and there may be two or three talkative ones, and if you pass close enough you will hear every topic of the times discussed or referred to, except those which are supposed to interest the poor. Wretchedness, poverty, hunger and distress are seldom mentioned. The possibilities of a match between prize-ring favorites, the day's evidence in the latest murder trial, the chance of war somewhere, the latest improvements in automobiles, a flying machine, the prosperity or depression of some other portion of the world, or the mistakes of the government at Washington—these, or others like them, are the topics of whatever conversation is held. It is for the most part a rambling, disconnected conversation.

"Wait until Dreyfus gets out of prison," said one to his little black-eyed neighbor one night, years ago, "and you'll see them guys fallin' on his neck."

"Maybe they will, and maybe they won't," the other muttered. "Them Frenchmen ain't strong for Jews."

The passing of a Broadway car awakens a vague idea of progress, and some one remarks: "They'll have them things runnin' by compressed air before we know it."

"I've driv' mule-cars by here myself," replies another.

A few moments before twelve a great box of bread is pushed outside the door, and exactly on the hour a portly, round-faced German takes his position by it, and calls: "Ready!" The whole line at once, like a well-drilled company of regulars, moves quickly, in good marching time, diagonally across the sidewalk to the inner edge and pushes, with only the noise of tramping feet, past the box. Each man reaches for a loaf and, breaking line, wanders off by himself. Most of them do not even glance at their bread but put it indifferently under their coats or in their pockets. They betake themselves heaven knows where—to lodging houses, park benches (if it be summer), hall-bedrooms possibly, although in most cases it is doubtful if they possess one, or to charitable missions of the poor. It is a small thing to get, a loaf of dry bread, but from three hundred to four hundred men will gather nightly from one year's end to the other to get it, and so it has its significance.

The thing that I protest against is that it endures. It would be so easy, as it seems to me, in a world of even moderate organization to do something that would end a spectacle of this kind once and for all, if it were no more than a law to destroy the inefficient. I say this not in cruelty but more particularly with the intention of awakening thought. There is so much to do. In America the nation's roads have not even begun to be made. Over vast stretches of the territory of the world the land is not tilled. There is not a tithe made of what the rank and file could actually use. Most of us are wanting strenuously for something.

A rule that would cause the arrest of a man in this situation would be merciful. A compulsory labor system that would involve regulation of hours, medical treatment, restoration of health, restoration of courage, would soon put an end to the man who is "down and out." He would of course be down and out to the extent that he had fallen into the clutches of this machine, but he would at least be on the wheel that might bring him back or destroy him utterly. It is of no use to say that life cannot do anything for the inefficient. It can. It does. And the haphazard must, and in the main does, give way to the well-organized. And the injured man need not be allowed to bleed to death. If a man is hurt accidentally a hospital wagon comes quickly. If he is broken in spirit, moneyless, afraid, nothing is done. Yet he is in far greater need of the hospital wagon than the other. The treatment should be different, that is all.

OUR RED SLAYER

IF you wish to see an exemplification of the law of life, the survival of one by the failure and death of another, go some day to any one of the great abattoirs which to-day on the East River, or in Jersey City, or elsewhere near the great metropolis receive and slay annually the thousands and hundreds of thousands of animals that make up a part of the city's meat supply. And there be sure and see, also, the individual who, as your agent and mine, is vicariously responsible for the awful slaughter. You will find him in a dark, red pit, blood-covered, standing in a sea of blood, while hour after hour and day after day there passes before him a line of screaming animals, hung by one leg, head down, and rolling steadily along a rail, which is slanted to get the benefit of gravity, while he, knife in hand, jabs unweariedly at their throats, the task of cutting their throats so that they may die of bleeding and exhaustion having become a wearisome and commonplace labor, one which he scarcely notices at all. He is a blood-red slayer, this individual, a butcher by trade, big, brawny, muscular, but clothed from head to foot in a tarpaulin coat and cap, which from long spattering by the blood of animals he has slain, have become this darksome red. Day after day and month after month here you may see him—your agent and mine—the great world wagging its way, the task of destroying life never becoming less arduous, the line of animals never becoming less thin.

A peculiar life to lead, is it not? One would think a man of any sensibility would become heartsick, or at the least, revolted and disgusted; but this man does not seem to be. Rather, he takes it as a matter of course, a thing which has no significance, any more than the eating of his food or the washing of his hands. Since it is a matter of business or of living, and seeing that others live by his labor, he does not care.

But it has significance. These creatures we see thus automatically and hopelessly trundling down a rail of death are really not so far removed from us in the scale of existence. You will find them but a little way down the ladder of mind, climbing slowly and patiently towards those heights to which we think we have permanently attained. There is a force back of them, a law which wills their existence, and they do not part with it readily. There is a terror of death for them as there is for us, and you will see it here exemplified, the horror that makes them run cold with the knowledge of their situation.

You will hear them squeal, the hogs; you will hear them baa, the sheep; you will hear the grinding clank of the chains and see the victims dropping: hogs, half-alive, into the vats of boiling water; the sheep into the range of butchers and carvers who flay them half-alive; while our red representative—yours and mine—stands there, stabbing, stabbing, stabbing, that we who are not sheep or hogs and who pay him for his labor may live and be merry and not die. Strange, isn't it?

A gruesome labor. A gruesome picture. We have been flattering ourselves these many centuries that our civilization had somehow got away from this old-time law of life living on death, but here amid all the gauds and refinements of our metropolitan life we find ourselves confronted by it, and here stands our salaried red man who murders our victims for us, while we look on indifferently, or stranger yet, remain blissfully unconscious that the bloody labor is in existence.

We live in cities such as this; crowd ourselves in ornamented chambers as much as possible; walk paths from which all painful indications of death have been eliminated, and think ourselves clean and kind and free of the old struggle, and yet behold our salaried agent ever at work; and ever the cry of the destroyed is rising to what heaven we know not, nor to what gods. We dream dreams of universal brotherhood and prate of the era of coming peace, but this slaughter is a stumbling-block over which we may not readily vault. It augurs something besides peace and love in this world. It forms a great commentary on the arrangement of the universe.

And yet this revolting picture is not without its relieving feature, though alas! the little softness visible points no way by which the victims may be spared. The very butcher is a human being, a father with little children. One day, after a discouraging hour of this terrible panorama, I walked out into the afternoon sunlight only to brood over the tragedy and terror of it all. This man struck me as a demon, a chill, phlegmatic, animal creature whose horrible eyes would contain no light save that of non-understanding and indifference. Moved by some curious impulse, I made my way to his home—to the sty where I expected to find him groveling —and found instead a little cottage, set about with grass and flowers, and under a large tree a bench. Here was my murderer sitting, here taking his evening's rest.

The sun was going down, the shadows beginning to fall. In the cool of the evening he was taking his ease, a rough, horny-handed man, large and uncouth, but on his knee a child. And such a child—young, not over two years, soft and delicate, with the bloom of babyhood on its cheek and the light of innocence in its eye; and here was this great murderer stroking it gently, the red man touching it softly with his hand.

I stood and looked at this picture, the thought of the blood-red pit coming back to me, the gouts of blood, the knife, the cries of his victims, the death throes; and then at this green grass and this tree and the father and his child.

Heaven forefend against the mysteries of life and its dangers. We know in part, we believe in part, but these things surpass the understanding of man and make our humble consciousness reel with the inexplicable riddle of existence. To live, to die, to be generous, to be brutal! How in the scheme of things are the conditions and feelings inextricably jumbled, and how we grope and stumble through our days to our graves!

WHEN THE SAILS ARE FURLED

THE waters of the open sea as they rush past Sandy Hook strike upon the northeasterly shore of Staten Island, a low-lying beach overshadowed by abruptly terminating cliffs. Northeastward, separated by this channel known as The Narrows, lies Long Island. As the waters flow onward, following the trend of the shore-line of Staten Island, they become less and less exposed to the winds of the sea, and soon, as they pass the northernmost end of the island, they make a sharp bend to the west, passing between it and Liberty Statue, where the tranquil Kill von Kull separates the island from New Jersey.

Long ere they reach this region the sea winds have spent their force, and the billows, which in clear weather are still visible far out, have sunk to ripples so diminutive that the water is not even disturbed. And here, in Staten Island, facing the Kill von Kull, still stands in almost rural quiet and beauty Sailors' Snug Harbor. Long ago this was truly a harbor, snug and undisturbed, a place where the storm-harried mariner, escaping the moods and dangers of the seven seas, found a still and safe retreat. To-day they come here, weary from a long life voyage, to find a quiet home. And truly it is restful in its arrangements. The grounds are kempt and green, the buildings pleasingly solemn, and the view altogether lovely, a mixture of land and sea.

In the early days this pleasantly quiet harbor was a

long distance from New York proper. Staten Island
was but thinly settled, and the Kill von Kull a passageway seldom used. To-day craft speed in endless procession like glorious birds over the great expanse of water.
On a clear day the long narrow skyline of New York is
visible, and when fogs make the way of the pilot uncertain the harbor resounds with endless monotony of fog-
horns, of vessels feeling an indefinite way.

Though the surroundings are pastoral, the appearance
of the inmates of this retreat, as well as their conversation, is of the sea, salty. Housed though they are for
the remainder of their days on land, they are still sailors,
vain of their service upon the great waters of the
world and but little tolerant of landlubbers in general.
To the passer-by without the walls they are visible lounging under the trees, their loose-fitting blue suits fluttering light with every breeze and their slouch hats
pulled rakishly over their eyes, an abandon characteristic of men whose lives have been spent more or less in
direct contact with wind and rain. You may see them
in fair weather pacing about the paths of the grounds,
or standing in groups under the trees. Upon a long
bench, immediately in front of the buildings, others are
sitting side by side, smoking and chatting. Many were
captains, not a few common sailors. But all are now so
aged that they can scarcely totter about, and hair of
white is more often seen than that of any other shade.

For a period of nearly a year—a spring, summer and
fall—I lived in the immediate vicinity of this retreat
and was always interested by the types of men finally
islanded here. They came, so I was told, from nearly

all lands, France, Germany, Sweden, Norway, Finland, Iceland, Spain, Austria, Russia, and elsewhere, though the majority chanced to be of English and American extraction. Also, I was told and can well believe they are, a restless if not exactly a troublesome lot, and take their final exile from the sea, due to increasing years and in most instances poverty, with no very great equanimity. Yet the surroundings and the provision made for them by the founder of this institution, who, though not a sea-faring man himself, acquired his fortune through the sea over a century ago, are charming and ample; but the curse, or at least the burden of age and the ending of their vigor and activities, rests heavily upon them, I am sure. I have watched them about the very few saloons of the region as well as the coffee-houses, the small lunch counters and the moving picture theaters, and have noted a kind of preferred solitude and spiritual irritability which spells all too plainly intense dissatisfaction at times with their state. Among the quondam rovers are rovers still, men who pine to be out and away and who chafe at old age and the few necessary restraints put upon them. They would rather travel, would rather have the money it costs to maintain them annually as a pension, outside, than be in the institution. Not many but feel a sort of weariness with days and with each other, and I am quite convinced that they would be happier if pensioned modestly and set free. Yet this is a great institution and indeed a splendid benefaction, but it insists upon what is the bane and destruction of heart and mind: conformity to routine, a monotonous system which wears as the drifting of water and eats as a worm at the heart.

And yet I doubt if a better conducted institution than this could be found, or one more suited to the needs and crotchets of so many men. They have ample liberty, excellent food, clothing and shelter, charming scenery, and all the leisure there is. They are not called upon to do any labor of any kind other than that of looking after their rooms and clothes. The grounds are so ample and the buildings so large that the attention of every one is instantly taken. As you enter at the north, where is the main entrance, there is a monument to Robert Richard Randall, the founder of the institution. This marks his final resting-place; the remains of the philanthropist were brought here from St. Mark's Church in New York, where they had lain since 1825.

The facts concerning the founding of this institution have always interested me. It seems that the father of "Captain" Robert Randall, the founder of the Harbor, was a Scotchman, who came to America in 1776 and settled in New Orleans. The Spanish Governor and Intendant of that city, Don Bernardo de Galvez, having declared the port open for the sale of prizes of Yankee privateers, Mr. Randall took an active interest in that great fleet of private-armed vessels whose exploits on the high seas, and even upon the coast of Great Britain itself, did much to contradict the modest assertion of the "British Naval Register" that:

"The winds and the seas are Britain's wide domain,
And not a sail but by permission spreads."

At his death his son Robert inherited the estate. Accustomed to come north to pass the summer months, Robert made, on one of his trips to New York, the acquaintance of a Mr. Farquhar, a man possessed of means but broken down by ill health. The mild climate of Louisiana agreed with the invalid, and a proposition to exchange estates was considered. After a bonus of five hundred guineas had been sent to Farquhar, this was effected. Mr. Randall then became a suburban resident of what was then the little city of New York. His property consisted of real estate fronting both sides of Broadway and adjacent streets, and extending from Eighth to Tenth Streets. At a distance of one-half mile to the westward, namely, near the site of the old Presbyterian Church on what is now Fifth Avenue, stood the dwelling of the Captain. Upon the piazza of this house, it is recorded, shaded by a luxuriant growth of ivy and clematis, the old gentleman was wont to sit in fine weather, with his dog by his side. Before the door were three rows of gladioli, which he carefully nurtured. He was a bachelor, and on the first day of June, 1801, being very ill and feeble but of "sound, disposing mind and memory," made his will. Alexander Hamilton and Daniel D. Tompkins drew up the papers. In this document he directed that his just debts be paid; that an annuity of forty pounds a year be given to each of the children of his half-brother until they were fifteen years old; a sum of one thousand pounds to each of his nephews upon their twenty-first birthday, and a like sum to his nieces on their marriage. He bequeathed to his housekeeper his sleeve-buttons and forty pounds, and to another servant his shoe and knee buckles and twenty pounds. When this had been recorded he looked up with an expression of anxiety.

"I am thinking," he said, "how I can dispose of the remainder of my property most wisely. What do you think, General?" turning to Hamilton.

"How did you accumulate the fortune you possess?"

"It was made for me by my father, and at his death became his sole heir."

"How did he acquire it?" asked Hamilton.

"By honest privateering," responded Randall.

"Then it might appropriately be left for the benefit of unfortunate and disabled seamen," volunteered Hamilton, and thereupon it was so bequeathed.

The early history of Snug Harbor is clouded with legal contests which covered a period of thirty years. Though at the time of the bequest Randall's property was of little value, being mostly farming land, situated on the outskirts of the populated parts of the city, the heirs foresaw something of its future value. In the National and State Courts they long waged a vigorous war to test the validity of the will. Their surmises as to the future value of the property were correct. For, although the income of the bequest was not more than a thousand a year at first, as the population of the city increased the rental rose by degrees, until in the present year it has reached a sum bordering $1,500,000, and the rise, even yet, is continuous.

However, the suits were eventually decided against the heirs, the court holding the will valid. As an institution the Harbor was incorporated in 1806, and the first building erected in 1831 and dedicated in 1833. So thirty years passed before the desire of a very plain-speaking document was carried into effect.

In the beginning there were but three buildings, which are to-day the central ones in a main group of nine. In toto, however, there are over sixty, situated in a park.

In a line, in the center of an eighteen hundred-foot lawn, stand the five main buildings, truly substantial and artistic. The view to the right and left is superb, tall trees shading walks and dividing stretches of lawn, with rows of benches scattered here and there. A statue by St. Gaudens beautifies the grounds between the main building and the governor's residence, while in another direction a fountain fills to the brim a flower-lined marble basin. Everywhere about the grounds and buildings are seen nautical signs and many interesting reminders of the man who willed the refuge.

The first little chapel that was built has long since been succeeded by an imposing edifice, rich in marbles and windows of stained glass. A music hall of stately dimensions, seating over a thousand people, graces a once vacant lawn. A hospital with beds for three hundred is but another addition, and still others are residences for the governor of the institution, the chaplain, physician, engineer, matron, steward, farmer, baker, and the buildings for each branch of labor required in the management of what is now a small city. In short, it has risen to the dignity of an immense institution, where a thousand old sailors are quietly anchored for the remainder of their days.

Some idea of the lavishness of the architecture can

be had by entering the comparatively new church, where marble and stained glass are harmoniously combined. The outer walls are pure white marble, the interior a soothing sanctuary of many colors. Underfoot is a rich brown marble from the shores of Lake Champlain. The wainscoting is of green rep and red Numidian marble. Eight immense pillars supporting the dome are in two shades of yellow Etrurian marble, delicate and unmarked. The altar is of the same shade, but exquisitely veined with a darker coloring. Both chancel and choir floors are richly mosaiced, the chancel steps being of the same delightful coloring as the piers. To the left of the chancel is the pulpit, an octagonal structure of Alps green, with bands and cornices of Etrurian and Sienna marble supported on eight columns of alternate Alps green and red Numidian, finished with a brass railing and Etrurian marble steps. The magnificent organ, with its two thousand three hundred or more pipes, is entirely worthy its charming setting. Over all falls the rich, warm-tinted light from numerous memorial windows, each a gem in design and coloring. On one of these the worshiper is admonished to ''Be of good cheer, for there shall be no loss of life among ye, but only of the ship.''

Admonish as one may, however, the majority of the old seamen are but little moved by such graven beauty; being hardened in simple, unorthodox ways. Not a few of them are given to swearing loudly, drinking frequently, snoring heavily on Sundays and otherwise disporting themselves in droll and unsanctified ways. To many of them this institution appears to be even a wasteful affair, intended more to irritate than to aid them. Not a few of them, as you may guess, resent routine, duty, and the very necessary officials, and each other. Although they possess comfortable and even superior living apartments, wholesome and abundant food, good clothing, abundant clean linen, a library of eight thousand volumes, newspapers, periodicals, time and opportunity for the pursuit of any fad or fancy, and no restrictions at which a reasonable man could demur, still they are not entirely happy. Life itself is passing, and that is the great sorrow.

And so occasionally there is to be found in that portion of the basement room from which the light is debarred, looking out from behind an iron door upon a company of blind mariners who occupy this section, working and telling stories, a mariner or two in jail. And if you venture to inquire, his mates will volunteer the information that he is neither ill nor demented but troubled with that complaint which is common to landsmen and sailors, "pure cussedness." In some the symptom of this, I am told, will take the form of an unconquerable desire to go from room to room in the early morning and pull aged and irate mariners from their comfortable beds. In others it has broken out as a spell of silence, no word for any one, old or young, official or fellow resident. In another drunkenness is the refuge, a protracted spell, resulting in dismissal, with an occasional reinstatement. Another will fight with his roommate or his neighbor, sometimes drawing a chalk line between the two halves of a double room and defying the other to cross it at peril of his life. There have been many public quarrels and fights. Yet, all things considered, and age and temperament being taken into consideration, they do well enough. And not a few have sufficient acumen and industry to enter upon profitable employments. For there are many visitors, to whom useful or ornamental things can be sold. And a few of these salts will even buy from or trade with each other.

In consequence one meets with an odd type of merchant here and there. There is one old seaman, for instance, a relic of Federal service in " '61," whose chamber is ornamented to the degree of confusion with things nautical, most of which are for sale. To enter upon him one must pass through a whole fleet of small craft, barks, brigs, schooners and sloops—the result of his jacknife leisure—arranged upon chests of drawers. Still another, at the time I visited the place, delighted in painting marine views on shells, and a third was fair at photography, having acquired his skill after arriving at the Harbor. He photographed and sold pictures of other inmates and some local scenes. Many can and do weave rugs and mats, others cane chairs or hammocks or fish-nets. Still others have a turn for executing small ornaments which they produce in great numbers and sell for their own profit. No one is compelled to work, and the result is that nearly all desire to. The perversity of human nature expresses itself there. In the long, light basement corridors, where it is warm and cozy, there are to be found hundreds of old sailors, all hard at work defying monotony with rapid and skilful finger movements.

All of these are not friendly, however, and many are vastly argumentative. No subject is too small nor any too large for their discussion in this sunlit forum. Especially are they inclined to belittle each other's experiences when comparing them with their own important past, and so many a word is passed in wrath.

"I hain't a-goin' to hear sich rubbish," remarked one seaman, who had taken offense at another's detailed account of his terrible experience in some sea fight of the Civil War. "Sich things ain't a-happenin' to common seamen."

"Yuh don't need to, yuh know," sarcastically replied the other. "This here's a free country, I guess, 'cept for criminals,—and they hain't all locked up, as they should be."

"So I thought when I first seed yuh," came the sneering reply, and then followed a hoarse chuckle which was only silenced by the stamping away of an irate salt with cheeks puffed out in rage.

Nearly all are irritatingly independent, resenting the least suggestion of superiority with stubborn sarcasm or indifference. Thus one, who owned his own ship once and had carefully refrained from whistling in deference to the superstitious line: "If you whistle aloud you'll call up a blow; if noisy you'll bring on a calm,'" met another strolling about the grounds exuberantly indulging a long-restrained propensity to "pipe the merry lay."

"I'll bet you wouldn't whistle aboard my ship," said he insinuatingly.

"Yeh! But I ain't aboard yer ship, thankee—I'm

on my own deck.'' And ''Haul in the bow lines; Jenny, you're my darling!'' triumphantly swelled out on the evening breeze.

Down on the unplaned planks of the Snug Harbor wharf a score of old salts, regardless of slivers, sit the livelong day and watch the white-winged craft passing up and down. Being ''square-riggers''—that is, having served all their lives aboard ship, barks and brigs— they look with silent contempt upon the fore and aft vessels of the harbor as they sail by. Presently comes, ''Hello, Jim! Goin' to launch her?'' from one who is contemplating with a quizzical eye a little weazened old man who comes clambering down the side of the dock with a miniature ship under his arm and a broad smile of satisfaction on his face.

''Ay, that's it,'' answers the newcomer. He has spent many weeks in building the little ship and now will be decided whether or not his skill has been wasted on a bad model. At once the critical faculty of the tars on the dock is engaged, and he of the boat becomes the subject of a brisk discussion. Sapient admonitions, along with long squirts of tobacco juice, are vouch-safed, the latter most accurately aimed at some neighboring target. Sarcasm is not wanting, the ability of the builder as well as the merit of his craft coming in for comment. The launching of such a craft has even engendered bitter hatreds and not a few fights.

We will say, however, that the craft is successfully launched and with sails full spread runs proudly before a light wind. In such a case invariably all the old sailors will look on with a keen squint and a certain tremor of satisfaction at seeing her behave so gallantly. Such being the case, the builder is at liberty to make a few sententious remarks anent the art of shipbuilding—not otherwise. And he may then retire after a time, proud in his knowledge and his very certain triumph over those who would have scoffed had they had the slightest opportunity.

I troubled to ask a number of these worthies from time to time whether, assuming they were young again, they would choose a sea-faring life. "Indeed I would, my boy," one answered me one morning. And another: "Not I. If I were to sail four thousand times I'd be as seasick the last trip as on the first day out. Every blessed trip I made for the first five years I nearly died of seasickness."

"Why did you keep it up, then?" I asked.

"Well, when I'd get into port everybody would ask: 'Well, how did you like it? Are you going again?' 'Of course I am,' I would answer, and went from pure shamefacedness and not to be outdone. After a while I didn't mind it so much, and finally kept to it 'cause I couldn't do anything else."

One of the old basket makers at the Harbor had occupied a rolling chair in the hospital and made baskets for nearly thirty-nine years. There was still another, ninety-three years of age, who would have been there forty years the summer I was there. And withal he was a most ingenious basket maker. One of the old salts kept an eating-stand where appetizing lunches were served, and he bore the distinction of having rounded the Horn forty-nine times in a sailing vessel. He was one of the few who possessed his soul in patience, resting content with his lot and turning to fate a gentle and smiling face. "Will you tell me of an adventure at sea?" I once asked him.

"I could," he answered, "but I would rather tell you of thirteen peaceful years here. I came here when I was seventy, though at sixty, when I was weathering a terrible storm around the Cape with little hope of ever seeing the rising sun, I promised myself that if ever I reached home again I would stay there. But I didn't know myself even then. My destiny was to remain on the sea for ten years more, with this Harbor for my few remaining years. At that, if I were young I would go to sea again, I believe. It's the only life for me."

Back of all this company of a thousand or more, playing their last parts upon this little Harbor stage, is an interesting mechanism, the system with which the institution is run. There is a clothing department, where the sailors get their new outfits twice a year. I warrant that the quizzical old salt who keeps it knows every rent and tear in every garment of the Harbor. There is a laundry and sewing department, of which the matron has charge. There is a great kitchen, absolutely clean, where is space enough to set up a score of little kitchens. At four p.m. there are visible only two dignitaries in this savory realm. At that time one slices tomatoes and the other "puts on tea" for a thousand, the number who regularly dine here. The labor of cutting great stacks of bread is done by a machine. Broiling steaks or frying fish for a thousand creates neither excitement

nor hurry. The entire kitchen staff numbers thirty all
told, and the thousand sailors are served with less noise
and confusion than an ordinary housewife makes in
cooking for a small family.

There are separate buildings devoted to baking, vegetable storing and so forth, and the steward, farmer,
baker and engineer, that important quartette, has each
his private residence upon the grounds. The hospital,
too, is a well-kept building, carefully arranged and
bright and cleanly as such institutions can be made.

Passing this place, I have often thought what a really
interesting and unique and beautiful charity it is, the
orderly and palatial buildings, the beautiful lawns and
flowers, and then the thousand and one characters who
after so many earthly vicissitudes have found their
way here and who, if left to their own devices, would
certainly find the world outside a stormy and desperate
affair. So old and so crotchety, most of them are. Where
would they go? Who would endure them? Wherewith
would they be clothed and fed? And again, after having
sailed so many seas and seen so much and been so independent and done heaven only knows what, how odd to
find them here, berthed into so peaceful a realm and
making out after any fashion at all. How quaint, how
naïve and unbelievable, almost. The blue waters of the
bay before them, the smooth even lawn in which the
great buildings rest, the flowers, the calm, the order, the
security. And yet I know, too, that to the hearts of all
of these, as to the hearts of each and every one of us,
come such terrific storms of restlessness, such light-
nings of anger or temper, such torturing hours of

ennui, beside which the windless lifelessness of Sargasso is as activity. How fierce their resentment of that onward shift and push of life that eventually loosens each and every barque from its moorings and sets it adrift, rudderless, upon the great, uncharted sea, their eyes and their mood all too plainly show. And yet here they are, and here they will remain until their barque is at last adrift, the last stay worn to a frazzle, the last chain rusted to dust. And betimes they wait, the sirenic call of older and better days ever in their ears—those days that can never, never, never be again.

Who would not be ill at ease at times? Who not crotchety, weary, contemptuous, however much he might choose to possess himself in serenity? There is this material Snug Harbor for their bodies, to be sure. But where is the peaceful haven of the heart—on what shore, by what sea—a Snug Harbor for the soul?

CHARACTERS

THE glory of the city is its variety. The drama of it lies in its extremes. I have been thinking to-day of all the interesting characters that have passed before me in times past on the streets of this city: generals, statesmen, artists, politicians, a most interesting company, and then of another company by no means so distinguished or so comfortable—the creatures at the other end of the ladder who, far from having brains, or executive ability, or wealth, or fame, have nothing save a weird astonishing individuality which would serve to give pause to almost the dullest. Many times I have been compelled by sheer astonishment to stop in the midst of duties that hurried me to contemplate some weird creature, drawn up from heaven knows what depths of this very strange and intricate city into the clear, brilliant daylight of a great, clean thoroughfare, and to wonder how, in all conscience, life had come to produce such a thing. The eyes of them! The bodies! The hats, the coats, the shoes, the motions! How often have I followed amazedly for blocks, for miles even, attempting to pigeonhole in my own mind the astonishing characteristics of a figure before me, attempting to say to myself what I really thought of it all, what misfortune or accident or condition of birth or of mind had worked out the sad or grim spectacle of a human being so distorted, a veritable caricature of womanhood or manhood. On

154

the streets of New York I have seen slipping here and
there truly marvelous creatures, and have realized instantly that I was looking at something most different,
peculiar, that here again life had accomplished an
actual *chef d'œuvre* of the bizarre or the grotesque or
the mad, had made something as strange and unaccount-
able as a great genius or a great master of men. Only
it had worked at the other extreme from public efficiency or smug, conventional public interest, and had
produced a singular variation, inefficient, unsocial, eccentric or evil, as you choose, qualities which worked to
exclude the subject of the variation from any participa-
tion in what we are pleased to call a normal life.

I am thinking, for instance, of a long, lean faced,
unkempt and bedraggled woman, not exceptionally old,
but roughened and hardened by what circumstances I
know not into a kind of horse, whom once of an early
winter's morning I encountered at Broadway and Fourteenth Street pushing a great rattletrap of a cart in
which was piled old rags, sacks, a chair, a box and what
else I know not, and all this with long, lean strides and
a kind of determined titan energy toward the North
River. Her body was clad in a mere semblance of clothing, rags which hung limp and dirty and close to her
form and seemingly wholly insufficient for the bitter
weather prevailing at the time. Her hair was coarse
and iron-gray, done in a shapeless knot and surmounted
by something in the shape of a small hat which might
have been rescued from an ashheap. Her eyes were fixed,
glassy almost, and seemingly unseeing. Here she came,
vigorous, stern, pushing this tatterdemalion cart, and

going God knows where. I followed to see and saw her
enter, finally, a wretched, degraded west side slum, in a
rear yard of which, in a wretched tumble-down tenement,
which occupied a part of it, she appeared to have a
room or floor. But what days and years of chaffering,
think you, were back of this eventual result, what years
of shabby dodging amid the giant legs of circumstances?
To grow out of childhood—once really soft, innocent
childhood—into a thing like this, an alley-scraping horse
—good God!

And then the men. What a curious company they
are, just those few who stand out in my memory, whom,
from a mere passing opportunity to look upon, I have
never been able to forget.

Thus, when I first came to New York and was on *The
World* there came into the reportorial room one cold
winter's night a messenger-boy, looking for a certain
reporter, for whom he had a message, a youth who positively was the most awkward and misshapen vehicle for
the task in hand that I have ever seen. I should say
here that whatever the rate of pay now, there are many
who will recall how little they were paid and how poorly
they were equipped—a tall youth, for instance, with a
uniform and cap for one two-thirds his size; a short one
with trousers six inches too long and gathered in plen-
teous folds above his shoes, and a cap that wobbled
loosely over his ears; or a fat boy with a tight suit, or a
lean boy with a loose one. Parsimony and indifference
were the outstanding characteristics of the two most
plethoric organizations serving the public in that field.

But this one. He was eighteen or nineteen (as contrasted with others of this same craft who were in the room at this very time, and who were not more than twelve or thirteen; that was before the child-labor laws), and his face was too large, and misshapen, a grotesquerie of the worst invention, a natural joke. His ears were too big and red, his mouth too large and twisted, his nose too humped and protruding, and his square jaw stood out too far, and yet by no means forcefully or aggressively. In addition, his hair needed cutting and stuck out from underneath his small, ill-fitting cap, which sat far up on the crown of his head. At the same time, his pants and coat being small, revealed extra lengths of naked red wrist and hands and made his feet seem even larger than they were.

In those days, as at present, it was almost a universal practice to kid the messenger-boy, large or small, whoever and wherever he was—unless, as at times he proved to be, too old or weary or down on his luck; and even then he was not always spared. In this instance it chanced that the reporter for whom this youth was looking was seated at a desk with myself and some others. We were chatting and laughing, when suddenly this apparition appeared.

"Why, hello Johnnie!" called the one addressed, turning and taking the message yet finding time to turn on the moss-covered line of messenger-boy humor. "Just in from the snow, are you? The best thing is never to get a hair-cut in winter. Positively, the neck should be protected from these inclement breezes."

"A little short on the pants there, James," chipped in a second, "but I presume the company figures that the less the baggage or equipment the greater the speed, eh?''

"In the matter of these suits," went on a third, "style and fit are necessarily secondary to sterling spiritual worth.''

"Aw, cut it!" retorted the youth defiantly.

Being new to New York and rather hard-pressed myself, I was throughout this scene studying this amazing figure and wondering how any corporation could be so parsimonious as to dress a starveling employee in so shabby a way, and from what wretched circumstances such a youth, who would endure such treatment and such work, must spring. Suddenly, seeing me looking at him and wondering, and just as the recipient of the message was handing him back his book signed, his face became painfully and, as it seemed to me, involuntarily contorted with such a grimace of misery and inward spiritual dissatisfaction as I had not seen anywhere before. It was a miserable and moving grimace, followed by a struggle not to show what he felt. But suddenly he turned and drawing a big red cold wrist and hand across his face and eyes and starting for the door, he blurted out: "I never did have no home, God damn it! I never did have no father or mother, like you people, nor no chance either. I was raised in an orphan asylum—" and he was gone.

"Sometimes," observed the youth who had started this line of jesting, getting up and looking apologetically at the rest of us, "this dam' persiflage can be sprung in the wrong place and at the wrong time. I apologize. I'm ashamed of myself, and sorry too."

"I'm sorry too," said another, a gentlemanly Southerner, whom later I came to know better and to like. But that boy!

For years, when I was a youth and was reading daily at the old Astor Library, there used to appear on the streets of New York an old man, the spindling counterpart, so far as height, weight and form were concerned, of William Cullen Bryant, who for shabbiness of attire, sameness of appearance, persistence of industry and yet futility in so far as any worth while work was concerned could hardly have been outclassed. A lodger at the Mills Hotel, in Bleecker Street, that hopeless wayplace of the unfortunate, he was also a frequenter of the Astor Library, where, as I came to know through watching him over months and years even, he would burrow by the hour among musty volumes from which he made copious notes jotted on paper with a pencil, both borrowed from the library authorities. Year after year for a period of ten years I encountered him from time to time wearing the same short, gray wool coat, the same thin black baggy trousers, the same cheap brownish-black Fedora hat, and the same long uncut hair and beard, the former curly and hanging about his shoulders. His body, even in the bitterest weather, never supported an overcoat. His hands were always bare and the wrists more or less exposed. He came invariably with a quick, energetic step toward the library or the Mills Hotel and turned a clear, blue, birdlike eye upon whomsoever surveyed him. But of ability—nothing, in so far as any one ever knew. The library authorities knew nothing of

anything he had ever achieved. Those who managed
the hotel of course knew nothing at all; they were not
even interested, though he had lived there for years.
In short, he lived and moved and had his being in want
and thinness, and finally died—leaving what? His
effects, as I was informed afterwards by the attendants
of the "hotel" which had housed him for years, consisted of a small parcel of clothes, worthless to any save
himself, and a box of scribbled notes, relating to what
no one ever knew. They were disjointed and mean-
ingless scraps of information, I was told, and dumped
out with the ashes after his demise. What, think you,
could have been his import to the world, his message?

And then Samuel Clampitt—or so a hand-lettered
scrawl over his gate read—whc maintained a junk-yard
near the Harlem River and One Hundred and Thirty-
eighth Street. He was a little man, very dark, very
hunched at the shoulders, with iron-gray hair, heavy,
bushy, black eyebrows, a very dark and seamy skin, and
hands that were quite like claws. He bought and sold
—or pretended to—old bottles, tin, iron, rags, and the
like. His place was a small yard or space of ground
lying next to a coal-yard and adjoining the river, and
about this he had built, or had found there, a high
board fence. And within, whenever the gates were
opened and one was permitted to look in, were collections of junk about as above tabulated, with, in addition,
some bits of iron fencing, old window-frames, part of
stair railings, gasoliers and the like. He himself was
rarely to be seen; I saw him no more than four or five

times during a period of three years in which I passed his yard daily. But, having occasion once to dispose of a collection of waste rags and clothing, I eventually sought him out and found him, after trying his gate on an average of once every two days during a period of two weeks and more. The thing that interested me from the first was that my tentative knockings at his gate, which was always closed and very high, were greeted by savage roars from several Great Danes that were far within and that pawed the high gate whenever I touched it or knocked. Yet eventually I did find him, the gate being open and the dogs chained and he inside. He was sitting in a dark corner of his little hut inside the yard, no window or door giving onto the street, and eating from a discolored tin pan on his lap which held a little bread, a tomato and some sausage. The thing that interested me most (apart from the fact that he appeared to me more of a gnome than a man) was these same dogs, now chained to a post a score of feet from me and most savagely snarling and charging as I talked. They were so savage and showed such great, white, glistening teeth that I was eager to retreat without waiting to complete my errand. However, I managed to explain my purpose—but to no result. He was not interested in my collection of junk, saying that he only bought material that was brought to him.

But the voice, so cracked and wheezy. And the eyes, shining like sparks of light under his heavy brows. And the thin, parchment-like, claw-like hands. He rasped irritatingly with his throat whenever he talked, before and after each word or sentence—"eck—eck—eck—I don't go out to buy stuff—eck—eck—eck. I only buy what's brought here—eck—eck—eck. I don't want any old rags—eck—eck—eck—I have more than I can sell now—eck—eck—eck.'' Then he fell to munching again.

"Those look like savage dogs," I ventured, hoping to lure him into a conversation.

It was not to be.

"Eck—eck—eck—they need to be—eck—eck—eck." That was all. He fell silent and would say no more.

I went out, curious as to what sort of a business this was, anyhow, and leaving him to himself.

But one morning, months later, turning a corner near there, a region of empty lots and some old sealed and untenanted storehouses, I found a crowd of boys following and stoning an old man who, on my coming near and then running to his rescue, I found to be this old dealer. He was attempting to hide behind a signboard which adjoined one of the storehouses. His face and hands were already cut by stones and bleeding. He was breathless and very much exhausted and frightened, but still angry and savage. ''They stoned me, the little devils—eck—eck—eck. They hit me with rocks—eck—eck—eck. I'll have the law on 'em, I will—eck—eck —eck. I'll get the police after 'em—eck—eck—eck. They're always trying to break into my place and I won't let 'em—eck—eck—eck.''

I wondered who could break into that place with those dogs loose, who would attempt it.

But that, as I found out later in conversation with boys of the vicinity, was just the trouble. At various times they had sought to enter to recover a tossed ball, possibly to steal something, and he had set the dogs (which were always unchained in his absence) on them; or, they had been attacked by the dogs and in turn had attempted to work him and them some injury.

Yet for a period of three years after this, to my knowledge, he continued to live there in that solitary place, harassed no doubt in this way. If he ever did any business I did not see it. The gates were nearly always closed, himself rarely to be seen.

Then one day a really terrible thing happened. Some children—not these same wicked boys but others less familiar with the neighborhood, I believe—were playing ball in an open space adjoining, and a fly being struck, the ball fell into the junk-yard. Three of the more courageous ones, as the papers stated afterwards, mounted the fence to see if they could get the ball, and one of them, more courageous than the others, actually leaped into the yard and was literally torn to bits by these same dogs, all but eaten alive. And there was no one to save him before he was dead. Old Clampitt was not there.

The horror was of course immediately reported to the police, who came and killed the dogs and then arrested Clampitt. A newspaper and police investigation of his life revealed nothing save that he was assumed to be an old junk-dealer who was eccentric, a solitary, without relatives or· friends. He claimed to have kept the ·dogs for protection, also that he had been set upon by youths of the vicinity and stoned, which was true. Even so, he was held for weeks in

jail pending this investigation of his connections. No
past crimes being found, apparently he was released.
But so terrified was he then by the furore his savage
dogs had aroused that he disappeared from this region
and was heard of no more. His old rag yard was
abandoned. But I often wondered about him afterwards,
the years he spent there alone.

And then *Old Ragpicker*, whom I have described in
Plays of the Natural and the Supernatural, and who
was as described.

And Hurstwood.

As interesting a type as I ever knew was an old
hunchback who, as I understood, had had a small music
business in the Bowery, years and years ago when that
street was still a vaudeville center, a sort of theatrical
Broadway.   Through experience he had come by a
little knowledge of popular songs and songbooks and
had engaged in the manufacture and sale of these
things.   But times changed and public taste varied and
he was not able to keep up with it all.   From little business to no business was an easy step, and then he failed
and took lodgings in one of the side streets off the
Bowery, below Fourth Street, eking out a precarious
existence, heaven only knows how.   Age had hounded
him even more than ill success.   His naturally dark skin
darkened still further and his black eyes retreated into
gloomy sockets.   I used to see him at odd times, at a
period when I lived in a vicinity near the Bowery, wend-
ing a lonely way through the crowded streets there, but
never until he accosted me one night in the dark did

I realize that he had become a beggar. A mumbled apology about hunger, a deprecating, shamefaced cough, and he was off again, the richer for a dime. In this case, time, to say nothing of life, had worked one of those disturbing grotesqueries which arrest one. He was so very somber, furtive, misshapen and lean, a veritable masque of a man whose very glance indicated inconsolable disappointment and whose presence, to many, would most certainly have come as an omen of failure. A hall-bedroom, a lodging-house cot, an occasional meal, some hidden corner in which to be at peace, in which to brood, and then a few years later he was found dead, alone, seated before a small table, his head leaning upon his arms in the shabby little room in which he dwelt. I know this to be true, for from time to time I made effort to hear of him. What, think you, would he have to say to his Creator if he might?

And yet another character. One day I was walking in Brooklyn in a very conservative neighborhood, when I saw what I fancied I never should see, in America, a woman furtively picking a piece of bread out of a garbage can. I had read of such things in Balzac, Hugo, Dickens—but where else? And she was not absolutely wretchedly dressed, though her appearance was far from satisfactory, and she had a tense expression about her face which betokened stress of some kind. My astonishment was such that I walked deliberately up to her and asked: "What is the matter with you—are you hungry?"

She had hidden the bread under her shawl as I approached and may have dropped it as we walked, for

I did not see it again though her hands appeared. Yet she refused to indulge in any conversation which would explain.

"I'm all right," she replied.

"But I saw you taking a piece of bread out of that can?"

"No."

"Don't you want any money?"

"No."

She appeared to be confused and walked away from me, edging toward the lines of fences to avoid contact. I put my hand in my pocket to offer a coin, but she hurried on. There was nothing to do but let her go her way—a thing which seemed intensely cruel, though there was apparently nothing else to do. I have often thought of this one, dark, tense, dreary, and half wondered whether it was all a dream or whether I really saw it.

But the city for me, in my time, has been flecked with these shadows of disaster in the guise of decayed mortals who stared at me out of hollow eyes in the midst of the utmost gayety. You turn a corner laughing amid scenes of enthusiasm and activity, perhaps, and here comes despair along, hooded and hollow-eyed, accusing you of undue levity. You dine at your table, serene in your moderate prosperity, and in looks want, thin-lipped, and pale, asking how can you eat when she is as she is. You feel the health and vigor of your body, warmly clad, and lo, here comes illness or weakness, thin and pining, and with cough or sigh or halting step, cries: "See how I suffer—and you—you have health!" Weakness confronts strength, poverty wealth, health sickness, courage cowardice, fortune the very depths of misfortune, and they know each other not—or defy each other. Of a truth, they either despise or fear, the one the other.

THE BEAUTY OF LIFE

THE beauty of life is involved very largely with the outline of its scenery. There are many other things which make up the joy of our world for us, but this is one of the most salient of its charms. The stretch of a level valley, the graceful rise of a hill, water running, a clump or a forest of trees—these add to the majesty of our being and show us how great a thing our world really is.

The significance of scenes in general which hold and bind our lives for us, making them sweet or grim according to the sharpness of our perceptions, is a wonderful thing. We are passing among them every moment. A new arrangement is had with every move we make. If we but lift our eyes we see a variation which is forever interesting and forever new.

The fact significant is that every scene possesses that vital instability which is the charm of existence. It is forever changing. The waters are running, the winds blowing, the light waxing and waning, and in the very ground such currents are at work as produce and modify all the visible life and color that we know. Great forces are at work, strong ones, and our own little lives are but a shadow of something that wills activity and enjoys it, that wills beauty and is beauty. The scenes that we see are purely representative of that.

But how, in the picturing of itself to itself, is the spirit of the universe revealed to us? Here are forces which at bottom might be supposed to be anything—grim, deadly, terrible—but on the surface how fair is their face. The trees are beautiful—you would not suppose there was anything deadly at work to create them. The water is mellifluent, sweet—you could hardly assume that it was grim in purpose or design. Every aspect of the scene reveals something pleasing which could scarcely have been the result of a cruel tendency, and yet we know that cruelty exists, or if not cruelty at least a tendency to contention—one thing striving with another and wearing it away, feeding upon it, destroying it which is productive of pain. And this element of contention represents all the cruelty there is. And this is not what is generally revealed in any scene.

Before such a picture of combined beauty and contentiousness—however graceful—life living upon life, in order to produce at least a part of this beauty—the mind pauses, wondering. It is so useless to quarrel with an order which is compulsory and produces all that we know of either joy or pain. This scene, as we look at it, is one of the joys, one of the compensations, of our existence which we must take whether we will or no, and which satisfies us whether or not we are aware of the contentiousness beneath. Even the contentiousness cannot be wholly sneered at or regretted, for at worst it produces the change which produces the other scenes and variations of which our world is full, and at worst it gives our life the edge of drama and tragedy, to say nothing of those phases of our moods which make our world seem beautiful.

Pity the mind for whom the immediate scene, involved as it is with change and decay and contentiousness, has no direct appeal, for whom the clouds hanging in the heavens, the wind stirring in the trees, the genial face of the earth, spread before the eye, has no meaning. Here are the birds daily circling in the air; here are the waters running in a thousand varied forms; here are the houses, the churches, the factories, and all their curious array of lines, angles, circles, cones, or towers, shafts and pinnacles which form ever new and pleasing combinations to which the mind, confused by other phases of life, can still turn for both solace and delight. For one not so mentally equipped a world of imagery is closed, with all that that implies: poetry, art, literature—one might almost say religion, for upon so much that is beautiful in nature does religion depend. To be dull to the finer beauties of line and curve that are forever beating upon the heart and mind—in earth, in air, in water, in sky or space—how deadly! The dark places of the world are full of that. Its slums and depths reek with the misery that knows no response to the physical beauty of nature, the wonder of its forms. To perceive these, to see the physical face of life as beautiful, to respond in feeling to the magnificent panoramas from which the eye cannot escape, is to be at once strong and wise mentally and physically, to have in the very blood and brain the beauty, glory and power of all that ever was or will be here on this earth.

A WAYPLACE OF THE FALLEN

In the center of what was once a fashionable section of New York, but is now a badly deteriorated tenement region, stands a hotel which to me is one of the curiosities of New York. It is really not a hotel at all, in one sense, and yet in another it is, a hybrid or cross between a hotel and a charity, one of those odd philanthropies of the early years following nineteen hundred, which were supposed to bridge with some form of relief the immense gap that existed between the rich and the poor; a gap that was not supposed to exist in a republic devoted to human brotherhood and the equality of man.

Let that be as it will. Exteriorly at least it is really a handsome affair, nine stories in height, with walls of cream-colored brick and gray stone trimmings, and a large, overhanging roof of dark-red curved tiles which suggests Florence and the South. Set apart in an open space it would be admirable. It is not, however, as its appearance would indicate, a hotel of any distinction of clientele, for it was built for an entirely different purpose. And, despite the aim and the dreams of those who sought to reach those who might be only temporarily embarrassed, rather than whose who were permanently so, and who might use this as a wayplace on their progress upward rather than on their way downward, still it is more the latter who frequent it most. It is really a rendezvous for those who are "down and out."

About the time that it was built, or a little after, I myself was in a bad way. It was not exactly that I was financially helpless or that I could not have come by relief in one and another form, if my pride would have let me, as that my pride and a certain psyche which, like a fever or a passion, must take its course, would not permit me to do successfully any of the things that normally I could and would have done. I was nervous, really very sick mentally, and very depressed. Life to me wore a somber and at most times a forbidding air, as though, indeed, there were furies between me and the way I would go. Yet, return I would not. And courage not lacking, a certain grim stubbornness that would not permit me to retreat nor yet to ask for help, at last for a brief period I took refuge here, as might one beset by a raging gale at sea take refuge in some seemingly quiet harbor, any port indeed, in order to forfend against utter annihilation.

And a strange, sad harbor I found it to be indeed, a nondescript and fantastic affair, sheltering a nondescript and quite fantastic throng. The thin-bodied and gray-bearded old men loitering out their last days here, and yet with a certain something about them that suggested courage or defiance, or at least a vague and errant will to live. The lean and down-at-heels and erratic-looking young men, with queer, restless, nervous eyes, and queer, restless, deceptive and nervous manners. And the chronic ne'er-do-wells, and bums even, panhandlers, street fiddle and horn players, street singers, street cripples and beggars of one kind and another. Some of them I had even encountered in the streets in my more prosperous hours and had given them dimes, and here I encountered them again. They were all so poor, if not physically or materially at least spiritually, or so nearly all, as to make contact with them disconcerting, if not offensive. For they walked, the most of them, with an air of rundown, hopeless inadequacy that was really disturbing to look upon. All of them were garbed in clothing which was not good and yet which at all times could not be said to be absolutely ragged. Rather, in many cases it was more of an intermediate character, such as you might expect to find on a person who was out of a job but who was still struggling to keep up appearances.

You would find, for instance, those whose suits were in a fair state of preservation but whose shoes were worn or torn. Again, there were those whose hats and shoes were good but whose trousers were worn and frayed. Still others would show a good pair of trousers or a moderately satisfactory coat, but such a gleam of wretched linen or so poor and faded a tie, that one was compelled to notice it. And the mere sight of it, as they themselves seemed to realize by their furtive efforts at concealment, was sufficient to convict them of want or worse. Between these grades and conditions there were so many other little gradations, such as the inadvertently revealed edge of a cotton shirt under a somewhat superior suit, the exposed end of a rag being used for a handkerchief, the shifting edge of a false shirt front, etc., so that by degrees one was moved to either sympathy or laughter, or both.

And the nature of the life here. It was such as to

preclude any reasonable classification from the point of view, say, of happiness or comfort. For all its exterior pretentiousness and inner spaciousness, it offered nothing really except two immense lounging-rooms or courts about which the various tiers or floors of rooms were built and which rose, uninterrupted, to the immense glass roofs or coverings nine stories above. There were several other large rooms—a reading-room, a smoking-room—equipped with chairs and tables, but which could only be occupied between 9 a.m. and 10 p.m., and which were watched over by as surly and disagreeable a type of orderly or guard as one would find anywhere—such orderlies or guards, for instance, as a prison or an institution of charity might employ. In fact, I never encountered an institution in which a charge was made for service which seemed to me more barren of courtesy, consideration or welcome.

We were all, as I soon found, here on sufferance. During a long day that began between 9 a.m., at which hour the room you occupied had to be vacated for the day, and 5 p.m., when it might be reoccupied once more, and not before, there was nothing to do but walk the streets if one was out of work, as most of these were, or sit in one or another of these same rooms filled with these same nondescripts, who looked and emanated the depression they felt and who were too taciturn or too evasive or shy or despondent to wish to talk to anybody. And in addition, neither these nor yourself were really welcome here. For, if you remained within these lobbies during the hours of nine and five daylight, these underlings surveyed you, if at all, with looks of indifference or

contempt, as who should say, ''Haven't you anything at
all to do?'' and most of those with whom you were in
contact could not help but feel this. It was too obvious
to be mistaken.

But to return to the type of person who came here
to lodge. Where did they all come from? one was
compelled to ask oneself. How did it happen that they
were so varied as to age, vigor or the lack of it and the
like? For not all were old or sick or poorly dressed.
Some quite the contrary. And yet how did some of them
manage to subsist, even with the aid of such a place as
this? What was before them? These thoughts, somehow,
would intrude themselves whether one would or no. For
some of them were so utterly hopeless looking. And
others (I told myself) were the natural idlers of the
world, or what was left of them, men too feeble, too
vagrom in thought, or too indifferent to make an earnest
effort in any direction. At least there was the possibility of many such being here. Again, there were
those of better mood and substance, like myself, say,
who were here because of stress, and who were temporarily driven to this form of economy, wretched as
it was. Others were obviously criminals or drug fiends,
or those suffering from some incurable or wasting disease,
who probably had little money and no strength, or
very little, and who were seeking to hide themselves
away here, to rest and content themselves as obscurely
and as cheaply as possible. (The maximum charges for
a room and a free bath in the public bathroom, the same
including towels and soap, ranged from twenty-five to
forty cents a day. A meal in the hotel dining-room, such

as it was, was fifteen cents. I ate several there.) Pick-pockets and thugs from other cities drifted in here, and it was not difficult to pick out an occasional detective studying those who chose to stay here. For the rest, they were of the flotsam and jetsam of all metropolitan life—the old, the young, the middle-aged, the former and the latter having in the main passed the period of success without achieving anything, the others waiting and drifting, perhaps until they should come upon something better. Some of them looked to me to be men who had put up a good fight, but in vain. Life had worsted them. Others looked as though they had not put up any fight at all.

And, again, the nature of the rooms here offered (one of which I was compelled to accept), the air or illusion of cells in an institution or prison that characterized them! They were really not rooms at all, as I found, but cells partitioned or arranged in such a way as to provide the largest amount of renting space and personal supervision and espionage to the founder and manager but only a bare bed to the guest. As I have said, they were all arranged either about an inner court or the exterior walls, so as to have the advantage of interior or exterior lighting, quite as all hotels and prisons are arranged. But the size of them and the amazingly small windows through which one looked, either into one or other of these courts or onto the streets outside! They were not more than five feet in width by eight in length, and contained each a small iron bed, a single chair, and a very small closet or wardrobe where some clothing might be installed, but so little that it could hardly be called a convenience.

And, again, the walls were really not walls at all, but marble partitions set upon iron legs or jacks two feet from the floor and reaching to within three feet of the ceiling, which permitted the observation of one's neighbor's legs from below, if you wished to observe those conveniences, or of studying his entire chamber if you chose to climb upon your bed and look over the top. These open spaces were of course protected by iron screens, which prevented any one entering save through the door.

It is obvious that any such arrangement would preclude any sense of privacy. When you were in your cell there came to you from all parts of the building the sounds of a general activity—the shuffling of feet, the clearing of throats, the rattling of dominoes in the reading-room below, voices in complaint or conversation, walkings to and fro, the slamming of doors here, there and everywhere, and what not. Coupled with this was the fact that the atmosphere of the whole building was permeated with tobacco smoke, and tainted or permeated with breaths in all degrees of strength from that of the drunkard to that of the drug fiend or consumptive. It was as though one were living in a weird dream. You were presumed to be alone, and yet you were not, and yet you were, only there was no sense of privacy, only a sense of being separated and then neglected and irritated.

And the way these noises and this atmosphere continued into the small hours of the morning was maddening. There is something, to begin with, about poverty and squalor that is as depressing and destructive as a gas or a chemic ferment. Poverty has color and odor and radiation as strong as any gas or ferment. It speaks. It mourns, and these radiations are destructive. Hence the instinctive impulse to flee not only disease but poverty.

At ten o'clock all lights in the lobbies and halls were supposed to be put out, and they were put out. There being none in the rooms, all was dark. Before this you would hear the shuffling of this throng bedward, and the piling of chairs on tables in the lobbies for the night in order that the orderlies of the hotel might sweep afterwards. There followed a general opening and shutting of doors and the sound made by individuals here and there stirring among their effects in the dark or straightening their beds. Finally, during the small hours of the night, when peace was supposed to reign, you would hear, whether you wished to or not, your neighbor and your neighbor's neighbor, even to the extent of aisles and floors distant, snoring and coughing or complaining. There were raucous demands from the irritated to "cut it out" or "turn over," and from others return remarks as "go to hell. Who do you think you are?"—retorts, sometimes brutal, sometimes merely irritable, which, however, kept the night vocal and one awake.

When, however, all these little difficulties had been finally ironed out and the last man had either quit grumbling or decided to dispose of his thoughts in a less audible way, there came an hour in which nature seemed truly able, even here, to "knit up the raveled sleeve of care.'' The noisy had now become silent, the nervous peaceful. Throughout the whole establishment an audible, rhythmic, synchronic breathing was now apparent. You felt as though some great chemic or psychic force were at work in the world, as though by some strange hocus-pocus of chemistry or physics, life was still capable of solving its difficulties, even though you were not, and as though these misfits of soul and body were still breathing in unison with something, as though silence and shadow were parts of some shrewd, huge plan to soothe the minds of the weary and to bring final order out of chaos.

In the morning, however, one awoke once more (at least I did) to a still more painful realization of what it means to be very poor. There were no conveniences, as I found, at least none which were private. Your bath was a public one, a shower only, one of a series of spouting discs in the basement, where you were compelled to foregather with others, taking your clothes with you—for unless you arose early you could not return to your room. The towels, fortunately, were separate, except for some roll-towels that served at washstands. The general toilet was either a long trough or a series of exposed closets, doorless segments extending along one wall. The shaving-room consisted of the mirrors above the washstands, nothing separate. Over all were the guards loitering to see that nothing was misused.

There is no question as to the necessity of such rigid, almost prison-like control, perhaps, but the general effect of it on one—or on me, let me say—was coarse and bitter.

"Blime me" (the attendants were for some curious reason mostly English), "you'd think there was no other time but nine for 'im to come start shaving. I say, you can't do that. We're closing 'ere now. Cut it out."

This to a shabby soul with a three days' growth of beard who has evidently not reached the stage where he understands the regulations of the institution.

"You'll 'ave to quit splattering water 'ereabouts, I'm telling you. This ain't no bawth. If you want to do that, go in the basement."

This to one who was not as careful about his shaving as he might be.

"You'll 'ave to be moving out o' 'ere now."

This to one who had fixed himself comfortably in the lobby and who might be in the way of some orderly who wanted to sweep or sprinkle a little sawdust. On every hand, at every time, as I noticed, it was the orderly or the hired servant, not the guest, who was the important and superior person. And it seemed to me, after a three days' study of it, that they were really looking for flaws and slight mistakes on the part of guests in order that they might show their authority and proclaim to the world their strength. It was discouraging.

The saddest part of it was that this place, with all its drawbacks, was still beyond the purse of many. Some, as anyone could see, only came here between the hours of ten in the morning and ten at night, the hours when lounging in these lobbies was permitted, to loaf and keep warm. They could not afford one of these palatial rooms but must only loaf here by day. It was at least warm and bright, and so, up to ten o'clock at night, not unsatisfactory. But having no room to go to at ten at night, they must make their way out. And this necessity, exposing them for what they were, bench-warmers, soon made them known to the guards or order-lies, who could be seen eyeing them, sometimes speaking to them, suggesting that they come no more, that they "cut it out." They were bums, benchers, really below the level of those who could afford to stop here, and so beneath that level of contempt which was regularly meted out to those who could stop here. I myself have seen them sidling or slipping out at 9:30 or 9:45, and with what an air—like that of a dog that is in danger of a booting. I have also seen a man at closing time count the remaining money in his possession, calculate a moment, and then rise and slip out into the night. Men such as these are not absolutely worthless, but they have reached the lowest rung of the ladder, are going down, not up, and beyond them is the Bowery, the hospital, and the river—the last, I think, the most merciful of all.

HELL'S KITCHEN

N. B. WHEN I first came to New York, and for years
afterward, it was a whim of the New York newspapers
to dub that region on the West Side which lies between
Thirty-sixth and Forty-first Streets and Ninth Avenue
and the Hudson River as *Hell's Kitchen*. There was
assumed to be operative there, shooting and killing
at will, a gang of young roughs that for savagery and
brutality was not to be outrivaled by any of the various
savage groups of the city. Disturbances, murders, riots,
were assumed to be common; the residents of this area
at once sullen and tempestuous. Interested by the stark
pictures of a slum life so often painted, I finally went
to reside there for a period. What follows is from
notes or brief pictures made at the time.

It is nine o'clock of a summer's evening. Approaching my place at this hour, suddenly I encounter a rabble
issuing out of Thirty-ninth Street into Tenth Avenue.
It is noisy, tempestuous, swirling. A frowsy-headed
man of about thirty eight, whose face is badly lacer-
ated and bleeding and whose coat is torn and covered
with dust, as though he had been rolling upon the
ground, leads the procession. He is walking with
that reckless abandon which characterizes the movements of the angry. A slatternly woman of doughy

complexion follows at his heels. About them sways a crowd of uncombed and stribbly-haired men and women and children. In the middle of the street, directly on a line with the man whom the crowd surrounds, but, to one side and nearer the side walk walks another man, undersized, thickset and energetic, who seems to take a great interest in the crowd. Though he keeps straight ahead, like the others, he keeps turning and looking, as though he expected a demonstration of some sort. No word is spoken by either the man or the woman, and as the curious company passes along under the variable glows of the store-lamps, shop-keepers and store-dealers come out and make humorous comments, but seem to think it not worth while to follow. I join the procession, since this now relates to my interests, and finally shake an impish, black-haired, ten-year-old girl by the arm until she looks up at me.

"What's the matter?"

"Aw, he hit him with a banister."

"Who hit him?"

"Why, that man out there in the street."

"What did he hit him for?"

"I dunno," she replies irritably. "He wouldn't get out of the room. They got to fightin' in the hall."

She moves away from me and I ply others fruitlessly, until, turning into Thirty-seventh Street, the green lights of the police station come into view. The object of this pilgrimage becomes apparent. I fall silent, following.

Reaching the station door, the injured man and his woman attendant enter, while the thickset individual who walked to one side, and the curious crowd remain without.

"Well?" says the sergeant within, glaring intolerantly at the twain as they push before him. The appearance of the injured man naturally takes his attention most.

"Lookit me eye," begins the wounded man, with that curious tone of injured dignity which the drunk and disorderly so frequently assume. "That—" and he interpolates a string of oaths descriptive of the man who has assaulted him "—hit me with a banister leg."

"Who hit you? Where is he? What did he hit you for?" This from the sergeant in a breath. The man begins again. The woman beside him interrupts with a description of her own.

"Shut up!" yells the sergeant savagely, showing his teeth. "I'll ram me fist down your throat if you don't. Let him tell what's the matter with him. You keep still."

The woman, overawed by the threat, stops her tirade. The man resumes.

"He hit me with a banister leg."

"What for?"

"It was this way, Captain. I went to call on this here lady and that —— came in and wanted me to get out of the room. I——"

"What relation is this man to you?" inquires the sergeant, addressing the woman.

"Nothin'," she replies blandly.

"Isn't the other man your husband?"

"No, he ain't, the blank-blank-blank-blank ——"

and you have a sweet string of oaths. "He's a ——,"
and she begins again to ardently describe the assailant.
The man assists her as best he can.

"I thought so," exclaims the officer vigorously. "Now,
you two get the hell out of here, and stay out, before I
club you both. Get on out! Beat it!"

"Ain't you goin' to lock him up?" demands the
victim.

"I lock nothing," vouchsafes the sergeant intolerantly. "Clear out of here, both of you. If I catch you
coming around here any more I'll give you both six
months."

He calls an officer from the rear room and the two
complainants, together with others who have ventured
in, myself included, beat a sullen retreat, the crowd
welcoming us on the outside. A buzz of conversation
follows. War is promised. When the victim is safely
down the steps he exclaims:

"All right! I ast him to arrest him. Now let 'em
look out. I'll go back there, I will. Yes, I will. I'll
kill the bastard, that's what I'll do. I'll show him
whether he'll hit me with a banister leg, the ——,"
and as he goes now, rather straight and yet rhythmically
forward, his assailant, who has been opposite him all
the while but in the middle of the street, keeps an equal
and amusing pace.

The crowd follows and turns into Thirty-ninth Street,
a half-block east of Tenth Avenue. It stops in front
of an old, stale, four-story red brick tenement. Some
of its windows are glowing softly in the night. On the

third floor some one is playing a flute. Quiet and peace seem to reign, and yet this——

"I'll show him whether he'll hit me," insists the injured man, entering the house. The woman follows, and then the short, thickset man from the street. One after another they disappear up the narrow stairs which begin at the back of the hall. Some of the crowd follows, myself included.

Presently, after a great deal of scuffling and hustling on the fourth floor, all return helter-skelter. They are followed by a large, comfortably-built, healthy, white-shirted Irish-American, who lives up there and who has strength and courage. Before him, pathetically small in size and strength, the others move, the mutilated and still protesting victim among them. Apparently he has been ejected from the room in which he had been before.

"I'll show him," he is still boasting. "I'll see whether he'll hit me with a banister leg, the ——."

"That's all right," says the large Irishman with a brogue, pushing him gently onto the sidewalk as he does so. "Go on now."

"I'll get even with him yet," insists the victim.

"That's all right. I don't care what you do tomorrow. Go on now."

The victim turns and looks up at this new authority fixedly, as though he knew him well, scratches his head and then turns and solemnly walks away. The other man does likewise. You wonder why.

"It's over now," says the new authority to the crowd, and he smiles as blandly as if he had been taking

part in an entertainment of some kind. The crowd
begins to dissolve. The man who drew the banister
leg or stick and who was to have been punished has also
disappeared.

"But how is this?" I ask of some one. "How can he
do that?"

"Him?" replies an Irish longshoreman who seems to
wish to satisfy my curiosity. "Don't you know who
that is? It's Patsy Finnerty. He used to be a champeen
prize-fighter. He won all the fights around here ten
years ago. Everybody knows him. He's in charge
over at the steamship dock now, but they won't fight
with him. If they did he wouldn't give 'em no more
work. They both work for him once in a while."

I see it all in a blinding flash and go to my own room.
How much more powerful is self-interest as typified by
Patsy than the police!

*   *   *   *   *

It is raining one night and I hear a voice in the room
above mine, singing. It is a good voice, sweet and clear,
but a little weak and faint down here.

> "Tyro-al, Tyro-al! Tyro-al, Tyro-al!
> Ich hab dich veeder, O mine Tyro-al!"

I know who lives up there by now: Mr. and Mrs.
Schmick and a little Schmick girl, about ten or eleven.
Being courageous in this vicinity because of the simplicity of these people, the awe they have for one who
holds himself rather aloof and dresses better than they,
and lonely, too, I go up. In response to my knock a
little fair-complexioned, heavily constructed German

woman with gray hair and blue eyes comes to the door.

"I heard some one singing," I say, "and I thought I would come up and ask you if I might not come in and listen. I live in the room below."

"Certainly. Why, of course." This with an upward lift of the voice. "Come right in." And although flustered and red because of what to her seems an embarrassing situation, she introduces me to her black-haired, heavy-faced husband, who is sitting at the center table with a zither before him.

"Papa, here is a gentleman who wants to hear the music."

I smile, and the old German arises, smiles and extends me a welcoming hand. He is sitting in the center of this combination sitting-room, parlor, kitchen and dining-room, his zither, inlaid with mother-of-pearl, on the table before him.

"I don't know your name," I say.

"Schmick," he replies.

I apologize for intruding but they both seem rather pleased. Also the little daughter, who is sitting in one corner.

"Were you singing?" I ask her.

"No. Mamma," she replies.

I look at the gray-haired little mother and she shows me even, white teeth in smiling at my astonishment.

"I sing but very little," she insists, blushing red. "My woice is not so strong any more."

"Won't you sing what you were singing just before I came in?" I ask.

Without any of that diffidence which characterizes so many of all classes she rises and putting one hand on the shoulder of her heavy, solemn-looking husband, asks him to strike the appropriate chord, and then breaks forth into one of those plaintive folksongs of the Tyrol which describes the longing of the singer for his native land.

"I have such a poor woice now," she insists when she concludes. "When I was younger it was different."

"Poor!" I exclaim. "It's very clear and beautiful. How old are you?"

"I will be fifty next August," she answers.

This woman is possessed of a sympathetic and altogether lovely disposition. How can she exist in Hell's Kitchen, amid grime and apparent hardness, and remain so sweet and sympathetic? In my youth and ignorance I wonder.

*   *   *   *   *

I am returning one day from a serious inspection of the small stores and shops of the neighborhood. As I near my door I am preceded up the street by three grimy coal-heavers, evidently returning from work in an immense coalyard in Eleventh Avenue.

"Come on in and have a pint," invites one great hulking fellow, with hands like small coal-shovels. He was, as it chanced, directly in front of my doorway.

One of his two companions needs no second invitation, but the other, a small, feeble-witted-looking individual, seems uncertain as to whether to go on or stay.

"Come on! Come on back and have a pint!" shouts

the first coal-heaver. "What the hell—ain't you no good at all? Come on!"

"Sure I am," returns the other diffidently. "But I ought to be home by half-past."

"Aw, home be damned! It won't take long to drink a pint. Come on."

"All right," returns the other, grinning sheepishly.

They go over the way to a saloon, and I pause in my own door. Presently a little girl comes down, carrying a tin pail.

"Whose little girl are you?" I inquire, not recognizing her.

"Mamma ain't home to-day," she returns quickly.

"Mamma?" I reply. "Why do you say that? I don't want your mamma. I live here."

"Oh, I thought you was the insurance man," she adds, grinning. "You look just like him."

"Aren't you the coal man's little girl?"

"Yes."

"Well, he just went into the saloon over there."

"Huh-uh. Mine's upstairs, drunk. He must be Mr. Kelly," and she goes quickly on with her bucket.

*   *   *   *   *

I am sitting in my room one night, listening to the sounds that float vaguely about this curious little unit of metropolitan life, when a dénouement in the social complications of this same coal-heaver's life is reached. I already know him now to be a rough man, for once or twice I heard him damning his children very loudly. But I did not suspect that there were likely to be complications over and above the world of the purely material.

"Die frau hat sich unbekommen!" ("The woman has taken her life!") I hear some one crying out in the hall, and then there is such a running and shuffling of feet and chattering that I open my door and join in the general hubbub. A score of tenants from the different floors are talking and gesticulating, and in the rear of the hall the door opening into the coal-heaver's dining-room is open. My landlady, Mrs. Witty, is on the scene, and even while we gaze a dapper little physician of the region, in a high hat and frockcoat, comes running up the steps and enters the open door in the rear.

"The doctor! The doctor!" The word passes from one to another.

"What is it?" I ask, questioning a little girl whom I had often seen playing tag on the sidewalk below.

"She took poison," she answers.

"Who?"

"That woman in there."

"The wife of the coal man?"

"Sure."

"What did she take it for?"

"I dunno. Here comes another doctor—look!"

Another young doctor is hurrying up the steps.

While we are still gaping at the opening and closing door, Mrs. Schmick, the little German woman who sang for me, comes out. She has evidently been laboring in the sick room and seems very much excited.

"Is she dead?" ask a half-dozen people as she hurries upstairs for something.

"No-oh," she answers, puckering up her mouth in her peculiar way. "She is very low, though. I must get some things," and she hurries away.

The crowd waits, and finally some light on the difficulty begins to break.

"She wouldn't live with him if he didn't stop going with her," my own landlady is saying. "I heard her say it."

"Who? Who?" inquires another.

"Why, that woman in Fortieth Street. You know her."

"No."

"Yes, you do. She lives next door to the blacksmith's shop, upstairs there, the woman with the two little girls."

"Her? Is that why she did it?"

"Sure."

"You don't say!"

They clatter on in this way and gradually it comes out in good order. This coal-heaver knows a widow in the next block. He is either in love with her or she is in love with him, and sometimes she comes here into Thirty-ninth Street to catch a glimpse of him. He has been seen with her a number of times and had been in the habit of driving his coal-wagon through Fortieth Street in order to catch a glimpse of her. His wife has frequently complained, of course, and there have been rows, bitter nocturnal wrangles, in which he has not come off triumphant. He has sworn and raved and struck his wife but he has been made to promise not to drive through Fortieth Street just the same. This day, however, he failed to keep this injunction. She was in Fortieth Street and had seen him, then had come home and in a fit of jealous rage and affectionate distemper had drunk a bottle of camphor. The husband is not home yet.

While we are still patiently awaiting him he arrives, dark, heavy, unprepared for the difficulty awaiting him, and very much astonished at the company gathered about his door.

"My wife!" he exclaims when told.

"Yes, your wife." This from several members of the company.

He hurries in, very shaken and frightened.

"What is this?" he demands as he passes the door and is confronted by serious-looking physicians. More we could not hear.

But after a time out he comes for something at the drugstore, then in again. He is in and out two or three times, and finally, before the assembled company and in explanation, wrings his hands.

"I never done nothin' to make her do this. I never done nothin'." He pauses, awaiting a denial, possibly, from some one, then adds: "The disgrace! I wouldn't mind if it wasn't for the disgrace!"

I meet Mrs. Schmick the next day in the hall. She has been indefatigable in her labors.

"Will she die?"

"No, she gets better now."

"Is he going to behave himself?"

She shrugs her shoulders, lifts up her hands dubiously.

"Mrs. Schmick," I ask, interestedly, her philosophy of life arresting me, "why do you work so hard? You didn't even know her, did you?"

"Ach, no. But she is sick now. She is in trouble. I would do as much for anybody."

And this is Hell's Kitchen, I recall.

*   *   *   *   *

Looking out of my front window I can see a great deal of all that goes on here, in connection with this house, I mean. Through the single narrow door under my window issue and return all those who have in any way anything to do with it. The mailman comes very seldom. There is a weekly life-insurance man who comes regularly, bangs on doors and complains that some people are in but won't answer. Ditto the gas man. Ditto the milkman. Ditto the collector for a rug and clock house. Many duns of many kinds who come to collect bills of all kinds and never can "get in." Of a morning only a half-dozen men and some six or eight girls seem to creep wearily and unwillingly forth to work. At night they and others, who have apparently other methods than that of regular toil for occupying their time, return with quite a different air. Truckmen and coalmen and Mr. Schmick arrive about the same time, half-past five. The son of a morose malster's clerk, who occupies the second floor rear, back of me, arrives at six. Beer-can carrying is the chief employment of the city cart-driver's wife, who lives on the third floor, the unemployed iron-worker, whose front room

I rent, and the ill-tempered woman with the three children on the fourth floor. The six or eight girls who go out evenings after their day's labor frequently do not begin to drift back until after eleven, several of them not before three or four. I have met them coming in. Queer figures slip in and out at all times, men and women who cannot be placed by me in any regular detail of the doings of this house. Some of them visit one or another of several "apartments" too frequently to make their comings and goings explicable on conventional grounds. It is a peculiar region and house, this, with marked streaks of gayety at times, and some very evident and frequently long-continued periods of depression and dissatisfaction and misery.

I am hanging out of my window one evening as usual when the keenest of all these local tragedies, in so far as this house and a home are concerned, is enacted directly below me. One of the daughters above-mentioned is followed down four flights of stairs and pushed out upon the sidewalk by her irate father and a bundle of wearing apparel thrown after her.

He is very angry and shouts: "You get out now. You can't come back into my house any more. Get out!"

He waves his arms dramatically. A crowd gathers. Men and women hang out of windows or gather closely about him and the girl, while the latter, quite young yet, perhaps fifteen, cries, and the onlookers eagerly demand to know what the trouble is.

"She's a street-walker, that's what she is," he screams. "She comes to my house after running around all night with loafers. Let her get out now."

"Aw, what do you want to turn her off for?" demands a sympathetic bystander who is evidently moved by the girl's tears. Others voice the same sentiment.

"You! You!" exclaims the old locksmith, who is her father, in uncontrollable rage. "You mind your own business. She is a street-walker, that's what she is. She shall not come into my house any more."

There is wrangling and more exclamations, and finally into the thick of the crowd comes a policeman, who tries to gather up all the phases of the story.

"You won't take her back, eh?" he asks of the father, after using all sorts of arguments to prevent a family rupture. "All right, then, come along," he says to the girl, and leads her around to the police station. "We'll find some place for you, maybe, to-night anyhow."

I heard that she did not stay at the station, after all, but what the conclusion of her career was, outside of the fact that the matter was reported to the Gerry Society, I never learned. But the reasons for her predicament struck me as obvious. Here was too much toil, too much gloom, too much solemnity for her, the non-appreciation which the youthful heart so much abhors. Elsewhere, perhaps, was light, warmth, merriment, beauty—or so she thought.

She went, she and so many others, fluttering eastward like a moth, into the heart of the great city which

lay mostly to the east. When she returned, and with
singed wings, she was no longer welcome.

*   *   *   *   *

But why they saw fit to dub it Hell's Kitchen, however, I could never discover. It seemed to me a very
ordinary slum neighborhood, poor and commonplace, and
sharply edged by poverty, but just life and very, very
human life at that.

A CERTAIN OIL REFINERY

THERE is a section of land very near New York, lying at the extreme southern point of the peninsula known as Bayonne, which is given up to a peculiar business. The peninsula is a long neck of land lying between those two large bays which extend a goodly distance on either hand, one toward the city of Newark, the other toward the vast and restless ocean beyond Brooklyn. Stormy winds sweep over it at many periods of the year. The seagull and the tern fly high over its darksome roof-tops. Tall stacks and bare, red buildings and scores of rounded tanks spread helter-skelter over its surface, give it a dreary, unkempt and yet not wholly inartistic appearance which appeals, much as a grotesque deformity appeals or a masque intended to represent pain.

This section is the seat of a most prosperous manufacturing establishment, a single limb of a many-branched tree, and its business is the manufacturing, or rather refining, of oil. Of an ordinary business day you would not want a more inspiring picture of that which is known as manufacture. Great ships, inbound and outbound, from all ports of the world, lie anchored at its docks. Long trains of oil cars are backed in on many spurs of tracks, which branch from main-line arteries and stand like caravans of steel, waiting to carry new burdens of oil to the uttermost parts of the land. There are many buildings and outhouses of all shapes and dimensions which are continually belching forth smoke in a solid mass, and if you stand and look in any direction on a gloomy day you may see red fires which burn and gleam in a steady way, giving a touch of somber richness to a scene which is otherwise only a mass of black and gray.

This region is remarkable for the art, as for the toil of it, if nothing more. A painter could here find a thousand contrasts in black and gray and red and blue, which would give him ample labor for his pen or brush. These stacks are so tall, the building from which they spring so low. Spread out over a marshy ground which was once all seaweed and which now shows patches of water stained with iridescent oil, broken here and there with other patches of black earth to match the blacker buildings which abound upon it, you have a combination in shades and tones of one color which no artist could resist. A Whistler could make wonderful blacks and whites of this. A Vierge or a Shinn could show us what it means to catch the exact image of darkness at its best. A casual visitor, if he is of a sensitive turn, shudders or turns away with a sense of depression haunting him. It is a great world of gloom, done in lines of splendid activity, but full of the pathos of faint contrasts in gray and black.

At that, it is not so much the art of it that is impressive as the solemn life situation which it represents. These people who work in it—and there are thousands of them—are of an order which you would call commonplace. They are not very bright intellectually, of course, or they would not work here. They are not very attractive physically, for nature suits body to mind in most instances, and these bodies as a rule reflect the heaviness of the intelligence which guides them. They are poor Swedes and Poles, Hungarians and Lithuanians, people who in many instances do not speak our tongue as yet, and who are used to conditions so rough and bare that those who are used to conditions of even moderate comfort shudder at the thought of them. They live in tumbledown shacks next to "the works" and they arrange their domestic economies heaven only knows how. Wages are not high (a dollar or a dollar and a half a day is good pay in most instances), and many of them have families to support, large families, for children in all the poorer sections are always numerous. There are dark, minute stores, and as dark and meaner saloons, where many of them (the men) drink. Looking at the homes and the saloons hereabout, it would seem to you as though any grade of intelligence ought to do better than this, as if an all-wise, directing intelligence, which we once assumed nature to possess, could not allow such homely, claptrap things to come into being. And yet here they are.

Taken as a mass, however, and in extreme heat or cold, under rain or snow, when the elements are beating about them, they achieve a swart solemnity, rise or fall to a somber dignity or misery for which nature might well be praised. They look so grim, so bare, so hopeless. Artists ought to make pictures of them. Writers ought to write of them. Musicians should get their inspiration for what is antiphonal and contra-puntal from such

things. They are of the darker moods of nature, its
meanest inspiration.

However, it is not of these houses alone that this
picture is to be made, but of the work within the plant,
its nature, its grayness, its intricacy, its rancidity, its
commonplaceness, its mental insufficiency; for it is a
routine, a process, lacking from one year's end to another any trace of anything creative—the filling of one
vat and another, for instance, and letting the same settle;
introducing into one vat and another a given measure of
chemicals which are known to bring about separation and
purifications or, in other words, the process called refining; opening gates in tubes and funnels which drain
the partially refined oils into other vats and finally into
barrels and tanks, which are placed on cars or ships.
You may find the how of it in any encyclopedia. But
the interesting thing to me is that men work and toil here
in a sickening atmosphere of blackness and shadow, of
vile odors, of vile substances, of vile surroundings. You
could not enter this yard, nor glance into one of these
buildings, nor look at these men tramping by, without
feeling that they were working in shadow and amid foul
odors and gases, which decidedly are not conducive to
either health or the highest order of intelligence.

Refuse tar, oil and acids greet the nostrils and sight
everywhere. The great chimneys on either hand are either
belching huge columns of black or blue smoke, or vapory
blue gases, which come in at the windows. The ground
under your feet is discolored by oil, and all the wagons,
cars, implements, machinery, buildings, and the men, of
course, are splotched and spotted with it. There seems

to be no escape. The very air is full of smoke and oil.

It is in this atmosphere that thousands of men are working. You may see them trudging in in the morning, their buckets or baskets over their arms, a consistent pallor overspreading their faces, an irritating cough in some instances indicating their contact with the smoke and fumes; and you may see them trudging out again at night, marked with the same pallor, coughing with the same cough; a day of peculiar duties followed by a night in the somber, gray places which they call home. Another line of men is always coming in as they go out. It is a line of men which straggles over all of two miles and is coming or going during an hour, either of the morning or the night. There is no gayety in it, no enthusiasm. You may see depicted on these faces only the mental attitude which ensues where one is compelled to work at some thing in which there is nothing creative. It is really, when all is said and done, not a pleasant picture.

I will not say, however, that it is an unrelieved hardship for men to work so. "The Lord tempereth the wind to the shorn lamb" is an old proverb and unquestionably a true one. Indubitably these men do not feel as keenly about these things as some of the more exalted intellectual types in life, and it is entirely possible that a conception of what we know as "atmosphere" may never have found lodgment in their brains. Nevertheless, it is true that their physical health is affected to a certain extent, and it is also true that the home life to which they return is what it is, whether this be due to low intelligence or low wages, or both. The one complements the other, of course. If any attempt were made to better their condition physically or mentally, it might well be looked upon by them as meddling. At the same time it is true that up to this time nothing has been done to improve their condition. Doing anything more for them than paying them wages is not thought of.

A long trough, for instance, a single low wooden tub, in a small boarded-off space, in the boss teamsters' shanty, with neither soap nor towels and only the light that comes from a low door, is all the provision made for the host of "still-cleaners," the men who are engaged in the removal of the filthy refuse—tar, acids, and vile residuums from the stills and agitators. In connection with the boiler-room, where over three hundred men congregate at noontime and at night, there is to be found nothing better. You may see rows of grimy men congregate at noontime and at night, to eat their lunch or dinner, there is to be found nothing better. You may see rows of grimy men in various departments attempting to clean themselves under such circumstances, and still others walking away without any attempt at cleaning themselves before leaving. It takes too long. The idea of furnishing a clean dining-room in which to eat or a place to hang coats has never occurred to any one. They bring their food in buckets.

However, that vast problem, the ethics of employment, is not up for discussion in this instance: only the picture which this industry presents. On a gray day or a stormy one, if you have a taste for the somber, you have here all the elements of a gloomy labor picture

which may not long endure, so steadily is the world
changing. On the one hand, masters of great force and
wealth, penurious to a degree, on the other the victims
of this same penuriousness and indifference, dumbly
accepting it, and over all this smoke and gas and these
foul odors about all these miserable chambers. Truly, I
doubt if one could wish a better hell for one's enemies
than some of the wretched chambers here, where men
rove about like troubled spirits in a purgatory of man's
devising; nor any mental state worse than that in which
most of these victims of Mother Nature find themselves.
At the bottom nothing but darkness and thickness of
wit, and dullness of feeling, let us say, and at the top
the great brilliant blooms known to the world as the
palaces and the office buildings and the private cars
and the art collections of the principal owners of the
stock of this concern. For those at the top, the brilliancy
of the mansions of Fifth Avenue, the gorgeousness of
the resorts of Newport and Palm Beach, the delights
of intelligence and freedom; for those beneath, the dark
chamber, the hanging smoke, pallor, foul odors, wretched
homes. Yet who shall say that this is not the fore-
ordained order of life? Can it be changed? Will it
ever be, permanently? Who is to say?

THE BOWERY MISSION

In the lower stretches of the Bowery, in New York, that street once famous for a tawdry sprightliness but now run to humdrum and commonplace, stands the Bowery Mission. It is really a pretentious affair of its kind, the most showy and successful of any religious effort directed toward reclaiming the bum, the sot, the crook and the failure. As a matter of fact, the three former, and not always the latter, are not easily reclaimed by religion or anything else. It is only when the three former degenerate into the latter that the thought of religion seems at all enticing, and then only on the side that leans toward help for themselves. The Bowery Mission as an institution gathers its full quota of these failures, and its double row of stately old English benches, paid for by earnest Christians who have heard of it through much newspaper heralding of its services, are nightly filled and overflowing.

The spirit of this organization is peculiar. It really does not ask anything of its adherents or attendants, or whatever they might be called, except that they come in. No dues are collected, no services exacted. There is even a free lunchroom and an employment bureau run in connection with it, where the hungry can get a cup of coffee and a roll at midnight and the jobless can sometimes hear of something to their advantage during the day. The whole spirit of the place is one of helpfulness, though the task is of necessity dispiriting and in some of its aspects gruesome.

For these individuals who frequent this place of worship are surely, of all the flotsam of the city, the most helpless and woebegone. There is something about the type of soul which turns to religion *in extremis* which is not pleasing. It appears to turn to religion about as a drowning man turns to a raft. There is the taint of personal advantage about it and not a little of the cant and whine of one who would curry favor with life or the Lord. Granting this, yet here they are, and here they come, out of the Bowery and the side streets of the Bowery, that wonderful ganglia of lodging houses; and in this place, and I presume others of its stripe, listen to presumably inspiring sermons. In all fairness, the speakers seem to realize that they have a difficult task to perform in awakening these men to a consciousness of their condition. They know that there is, if not cant, at least mental and physical lethargy to overcome. These bodies are poisoned by their own inactivity and sense of defeat. When one looks at them collectively the idea instinctively forces itself forward: "What is there to save?"

And yet, shabby and depressing as are these facts, there is a collective, coherent charm and color about the effort itself which to one who views it entirely disinterestedly is not to be scoffed at. The hall itself, a long deep store turned to a semblance of Gothic beauty by a series of colored windows set in the store-front facing the Bowery, and by a gallery of high-backed benches of Gothic design at the back, and by mottoes and traceries in dark blue and gold which harmonize fittingly with the walnut stain of the woodwork, is inviting. Even the shabby greenish-brown and dusty gray coats of the audience blend well with the woodwork, and even the pale colorless faces of gray or ivory hue somehow add to what is unquestionably an artistic and ornamental effect.

The gospel of God the All-Forgiving is the only doctrine here thoroughly insisted upon. It is, in a way, a doctrine of inspiration. That it is really never too late to change, to come back and begin all over, is the basic idea. God, once appealed to, can do anything to restore the contrite heart to power and efficiency. Believe in God, believe that He really loves you, believe that He desires to make you all you should be, and you will be. Your fortunes will change. You will come into peace and decency and be respected once more. God will help you.

It is interesting to watch the effect of this inspirational doctrine, driven home as it is by imaginative address, oratorical fire, and sometimes physical vehemence. The speakers, the ordinary religionists of an inspirational and moral turn, not infrequently possess real magnetism, the power to attract and sway their hearers. These dismal wanderers, living largely in doubt and despair, can actually be seen to take on a pseudo-courage as they listen. You can see them stir and shift, the idea that possibly something can be done for them if only they can get this belief into their minds, actually influencing their bodies. And now and then some one who has got a soft job, a place, through the ministrations of the mission workers, or who has been pulled out of a state of absolute despair—or at least claims to have been—will arise and testify that such has been the case. His long wanderings in the dark will actually fascinate him by contrast and he will expatiate with shabby eloquence upon his present decency and comfort as contrasted with what he was. I remember one night hearing an old man tell what a curse he had been to a kind-hearted sister, and how he wanted but one thing, now that he was coming out of his dream of evil, and that was to let her see some day that he had really reformed. It was a pathetic wish, so little to hope for, but the wish was seemingly sincere and the speaker fairly recovered.

And they claim to recover a percentage, small though it is, to actual service and usefulness. The service may not be great, the usefulness not very important, but such as it is, there it is. And if one could but believe them, so dubious is all so-called reformation of this sort, there is something pleasing in the thought that out of the muck and waste of the slough of despond some of these might actually be brought to health and decency, a worthwhile living, say. Yet are they? Dirty, grimy, like flies immersed in glue, can they be—have they ever been—dragged to safety and set on their feet again, clean, hopeful, or even weakly so?

I remember listening one night to the story of the son of the man who founded the mission. It appears that the father was rich and the boy indulgently fostered, until at last he turned out to be a drunkard, rake and what not—all the nouns usually applied to those who do evil. His father had tried to retain a responsible position for him among his affairs but was finally compelled to cut him off. He ordered him out of his house, his business, had his will remade, cutting him off without a dollar, and declared vehemently and determinedly that he would never look upon him again. The boy disappeared. Some five years later a thin, shabby, down-hearted wastrel strolled into the mission and sat down, contenting himself with occupying a far corner and listening wearily to what was being said. After the services were over he came to the director in charge and confessed that he was the son of the man who had founded the mission, that he was actually at the end of his rope, hungry, and with no place to sleep—your prodigal son. The director, of course, at once took him in charge, gave him a meal and a bed, and set about considering whether anything could be done for him.

It appears that the youth, like his prototype of the parable, had actually had his fill of the husks, but in addition he was sick and dispirited and willing to die. The director encouraged him to hope. He was young yet. There was still a chance for him. He first gave him odd jobs about the mission, then secured him a place as waiter in a small restaurant, and finally, figuring out a notable idea, took him to the foreman of the father's own printing establishment and asked a place for him as a printer's devil. The character of the mission director was sufficient guarantee and the place was given, though no one knew who the rundown assistant really was. Finally, after over eleven months of service, the director went to the owner of the business

and said: "Would you like to know where your
boy is?"

"No," the father replied sharply, "I would not."

"If you knew he had reformed and had been working
for at least a year and a half steadily in one place—
wouldn't that make any difference?"

"Well," he replied, looking at him quizzically, "it
might. Where is he?"

"Right here in your own establishment."

The old man got up. "What's he doing? Let me
look at him."

The two traversed the halls of a great business establishment and finally came to the department where the
youth was working. The father, eager but cautious,
scanned the room and saw his son, himself unnoticed.
He was sticking type, a green shade over his eyes.

For a moment the parent hesitated, then went over.

"Harry," he called.

The boy jumped.

"Father!" he cried.

It was described as a moment of intense emotion. The
boy broke down and wept and the father shed tears
over him. Finally he sobered himself and said: "Now
you come with me. I guess you're all right enough to be
my son again. You can set more type to-morrow." And
he led him away.

Truth? Or Romance? I do not know.

The final answer to this form of service, however, is
in the mission itself. Nightly you may see them rise
and hear them testify. One night the speaker, pouring
forth a fiery description of God's power, stopped in the

midst of his address and said: "Is that you, Tommy Wilson, up there in the gallery?"

"Yes, sir."

"Tommy, I'm glad to see you. Won't you get up and sing 'My Lord and I'? I know there isn't any one here who wouldn't rather hear you sing than me preach any time. Will you?"

"Yes, sir."

Up in the gallery, three rows back, there arose a shabby little man, his dusty suit showing the well-worn marks of age. He was clean and docile, however, and seemed to be some one whom the mission had reclaimed in times past. In fact, the speaker made it clear that Tommy was a great card, for out of the gutter he had come to contribute a beautiful voice to the mission, a voice that was now missing because he had a job in a faraway part of the city.

Tommy sang. He put his hands in his coat pockets, stood perfectly erect, and with his head thrown back gave vent to such a sweet, clear melody that it moved every heart. It was not a strong voice, not showy, but pure and lovely, like a limpid stream. The song he sang was this:

> I have a Friend so precious,
>   So very dear to me;
> He loves me with such tender love,
>   He loves me faithfully.
> I could not live apart from Him,
>   I love to feel Him nigh;
> And so we dwell together,
>   My Lord and I.

Sometimes I'm faint and weary,
  He knows that I am weak,
And as He bids me lean on Him
  His help I gladly seek;
He leads me in the paths of light,
  Beneath a sunny sky;
And so we walk together,
  My Lord and I.

I tell Him all my sorrows,
  I tell Him all my joys,
I tell Him all that pleases me,
  I tell Him what annoys;
He tells me what I ought to do,
  He tells me how to try;
And so we walk together,
  My Lord and I.

He knows how I'm longing
  Some weary soul to win,
And so He bids me go and speak
  The loving word for Him;
He bids me tell His wondrous love,
  And why He came to die;
And so we work together
  My Lord and I.

As he sang I could not help thinking of this imagi-
natively personified Lord of the Universe in all His
power and wisdom taking note of this singing, shabby
ant—of the faith that it required to believe that He
would. Then I thought of the vast forces that shift and
turn in their mighty inscrutability. I thought of suns
and planets that die, not knowing why they are born.
Of the vast machinery, the vast chemistry, of things
dark, ruthless, brutal, and then of love, and mercy and
tenderness that is somehow present along with cruelty
and savagery. And then I thought of this little, shabby

reclaimed water-rat, this scraping of the mud crawled
to the bank, who yet could stand there in his shabby
coat and sing! What if, after all, as the Christian Scien-
tists believe, the Lord was not distant from things but
here, now, everywhere, divine goodness speaking in and
through matter and man. What if evil and weakness
and failure were dreams only, evil dreams, from which
we wake to something different, better—Omnipotence, to
essential unity with life and love? For a moment, so
mysterious a thing is emotion and romance, the thought
carried me with the singer, and I sang with him:

> "And so we walk together,
> My Lord and I."

But outside in the cold, hard street, with its trucks
and cars, I knew the informing spirit is not quite like
that, neither so kind nor helpful—at least not to all.

THE WONDER OF THE WATER

I cross, each morning, a bridge that spans a river
of running water. It is not a wide river, but one popu-
lous with boats and teeming with all the mercantile
life of a great city. Its current is swift, its bottom
deep; it carries on its glassy bosom the freight of a
thousand—of ten thousand merchants. Only the conception of something supernally wonderful haunts me as I
cross it, and I gaze at the picture of its boats and
barges, its spars and sails, spellbound by their beauty.

The boats on this little river—the Harlem—traverse
the seven seas. You may stand and see them go by:
vessels loaded with brick and stone, with lumber and
cement, with coal, iron, lime, oil—a great gamut of
serviceable things which the world needs and which
is here forever being delivered or carried away.
These boats come from the Hudson and the Chesapeake,
from Maine, Florida, the Gulf of Mexico, Europe, Asia,
Africa and the rest of the world. They tie up to these
small docks in friendly rows and nose the banks in
silence, while human beings, honored only by being
allowed to guide and direct their stately proportions,
clamber over them.

It is not so much these boats, however, as it is the
water which curls under them, which sips and eddies
about the docks and posts, and circles away in spinning
rings, which takes my fancy. This water, which flows

here so swiftly, comes from so far. It has been washing about the world, lo, these many centuries—for how long the imagination of man cannot conceive. And here it is running pleasantly at my feet, the light of the morning sun warming it with amethystine beams and giving it a luster which the deeps of the sea cannot have.

This water, as it comes before me now, gives me the impression of having been a hundred and a thousand things, maybe—the torrent from the height, bounding ecstatically downward into the depths of some cavern, rolling in gloom under the immensity of the volume of the sea, or a tiny cloudlet hanging like a little red island in the sky, a dark thundercloud pouring its fury and wrath upon a luckless multitude. It may have been a cup of water, a glass of wine, a tear, a gush of blood—anything in the whole gamut of human experience, or out of it—and yet here for this hour at least it lies darkling and purling, murmuring cheerfully about these docks and piers. When you think of the steam that is made of it by heat, floating over our whole civilization like plumes; the frost of the windowpanes spread in such tropical luxury of a winter morning; the snow, in its forms of stars and flowers; the rich rains of summer, falling with such rhythmic persistence; and then the ice, the fog, the very atmosphere we breathe, infiltrated by this wonderful medium and were ourselves almost entirely composed of it, you see how almost mystic it becomes. We owe all our forms to it; the beauty of the flowers, the stateliness of the trees, the shape and grandeur of the mountains, all, in fact—our minds and bodies, so much water and so little substance.

And here it is under our bridge, hurrying away. It may be that it has mind, that in its fluid depths lie all the religions and philosophies of the world. Sweep us away, and out of it might rise new shapes and forms, more glorious, more radiant. We may not even guess the alpha of its powers.

I do not know what this green fluid is that runs between green banks and past docks and factories and the habitations of men. It has a life quality, and mayhap a soul quality, which I cannot fathom, but with each turn of its ripples and each gurgle of its tide the heart of me leaps like a voice in song. I can reason no more. It is too colorful, too rhythmic, too silent, not to call forth that which is deemed exaltation by the world, and I stand spellbound, longing for I know not what, nor why.

THE MAN ON THE BENCH

IT is nine o'clock of a summer's night. The great
city all about is still astir, active, interested, apparently
comfortable. Lights gleam out from stores lazily. The
cars go rumbling by only partially filled, as is usual
at this time of night. People stroll in parks in a score
of places throughout the city, enjoying the cool of the
night, such as it is.

In any one of these, as the evening wanes, may be
witnessed one of the characteristic spectacles of the
town: the gathering of the "benchers." Here, while
one strolls about for an hour's amusement or sits on a
bench, may be seen the man whom the city has beaten,
seeking a place to sleep.

What a motley company! What a port of missing
men! This young one who slips by me in shabby,
clay-colored clothes and a worn, dirty straw hat, is
only temporarily down on his luck, for he has youth.
It may be a puling youth, half-witted, with ill-conceived
understanding of things as they are, but it is youth,
with some muscle and some activity, and as such it is sal-
able. Some one will buy it for something for a little
while.

But this other thing that comes shambling toward
me, dirty, dust in its ears, dust in its eyes, dust in
its hair, a meager recollection of a hat, dull, hopeless,
doglike eyes—what has it to offer life? Nothing!
217

Practically so. An appetite which life will not satisfy, a racked and thin-blooded body which life cannot use, a rusty, cracked and battered piece of machinery which is fit only for the scrap-heap. And yet it lingers on, clings on, hoping for what? And this third thing—a woman, if you please, in rags and tatters, a gray cape for a shawl, a queer, flat, shapeless thing which she wears on her head for a hat, shoes that are not shoes but cracked strips of leather, a skirt that is a bag only, hands, face, skin wrinkled and dirty, yet who seeks to rest or sleep here the night through. And now she is stuffing old newspapers between her dress and her breast to keep warm. And enveloping her hands in her rag of a shawl!

Yet she and those others make but three of many, so grim, so strange, so shabby a company. What, in God's name, has life done to them that they are so cracked and bruised and worthless?

No heart, or not a good one perhaps, in any of these bodies; no stomach, or a mere bundle of distorted viscera; no liver or kidneys worthy the name, but only botched or ill-working organs of these names in their place; eyes poor; hearing possibly defective; hair fading; skin clammy. Merciful God! is it to this condition that we come, you and I, if life be not merciful?

I am not morbid. I know that men must make good. I know that to be useful to the world they must have a spark of divine fire. But who is to provide the fire? Who did, in the first place? Where is it now? What blew it out? The individual himself? Not always. Man is not really responsible for his actions. Society?

Society is not really responsible for itself or for its individuals. Nature? God? Very likely, although there is room for much discussion and much illumination here.

But before we point the finger of scorn or shrug the shoulder of indifference, one word: Life does provide the divine fire, and that free and unasked, to many. It does provide a fine constitution, and that free and unasked, to many. It does provide beauty—aye it pours it into the lap of some. Life works in the clay of its interests, fashioning, fashioning. With some handfuls it fashions lovingly, joyously, radiantly. It gives one girl, for instance, a passion for art, an ear for music, a throat for singing, a joy in humor and beauty, which grows and becomes marvelous and is irresistible. Into the seed of a boy it puts strength, suppleness, facility of thought, facility of expression, desire. It not infrequently puts a wild surging determination to do and be in his brain which carries him like powder a bullet, straight to the mark.

But what or who provided the charge of powder behind that bullet? Who fashioned the chorded throat? Who worked over this face of flowerlike expression, until men burn with wild passion and lay kingdoms and hierarchies and powers at its feet? We palaver so much of personal effort. We say of this one and that: He did not try. I ask you this: had he tried, what of it? How far would his little impulse have carried him? What would it have overcome? Would it have placed him above the level of a coal-stoker or a sand-hog? Would it have fitted him to contend with even these?

Would it have matched his ideas, or his ideas have matched it? Who? What? How? Dark thoughts!

"Ah!" but I hear you say, "that is not the question. Effort is the question, not where his effort will carry him." True. Who gave him his fitness for effort, or his unfitness? Who took away his courage? Why could it be taken? Dark thought, and still more dark the deeps behind it.

Here they are, though, pale anæmic weeds or broken flowers, slipping about looking for a bench to sleep on in our park. They are wondering where the next meal is coming from, the next job, the next bed. They are wondering whither they are going to go, what they are going to do, who is going to say something to them. Or maybe they are past wondering, past dreaming, past thinking over lost battles and lost life. Oh, nature! where now in your laboratory of dark forces, you plan and weave, be merciful. For these, after all, are of you, your clay; they need not be destroyed.

Yet meantime the city sings of its happiness, the lights burn, the autos honk; there are great restaurants agleam with lights and merriment. See, that is where strength is!

I like this fact of the man on the bench, as sad as it is. It is the evidence of the grimness of life, its subtlety, its indifference. Men pass them by. The world is elsewhere. And yet I know that below all this awaits after all the unescapable chemistry of things. They are not out of nature. They cannot escape it really. They are of it— an integral part of the great mystery and beauty—even they. They fare ill here, now, perhaps—very. Yet it is entirely possible that they need only wait, and life will eventually come round to them. They cannot escape it; it must use them. The potter has but so much clay. He cannot but mold it again and again. And as for the fire, He cannot ultimately prevent it. It goes, somewhat wild or mild, into all He does.

THE MEN IN THE DARK

I⊤ is not really dark in the accepted sense of the word, for a great, yellow, electric lamp sputtering overhead casts a wide circle of gold, but it is one-fifteen of a cold January morning, and this light is all the immediate light there is. The offices of the great newspaper center, the sidewalk in front of one of which constitutes the stage of this scene, are dark and silent. The great presses in every newspaper building hereabouts are getting ready to whir mightily, and if only the passers-by would cease their shuffling you could hear the noises of preparation. A little later, when they are actually in motion, you can hear them, a sound of rushing, dim and muffled, but audible—the cataract of news which the world waits for, its daily mental stimulus, not unlike the bread that is left at your door for your body.

But who are these peculiar individuals who seem to be gathering here at this time in the morning? You did not notice any one a few minutes ago, but now there are three or four over there discussing the reasons for the present hard times, and here in the shadow of this great arch of a door are three or four more. And now you look about you and they are coming from all directions, slipping in out of the shadow toward this light, where sits a fat old Irish woman beside an empty news-stand waiting to tend it, for as yet there is nothing on it. They all seem at first to be men of one type, small and under-weight and gaunt. But a little later you realize that they are not so much alike in height and weight as you first thought, and of differing nationalities. But they are all cold, though, that is certain, and a little impatient. They are constantly shifting and turning and looking at the City Hall clock, where its yellow face shows the hour, or looking down the street, and sometimes murmuring, but not much. There is very little said.

"What is all the trouble?" you ask of some available bystander, who ought to be fairly *en rapport* with the situation, since he has been standing here for some time.

"Nothin'," he retorts. "They're waitin' for the mornin' papers. They're lookin' to see which can git to a job first."

"Oh!" you exclaim, a great light breaking. "So they're here to get a good start. They wait all night, eh? That's pretty tough, isn't it?"

"Oh, I don't know. They're mostly Swedes and Germans." This last as though these two nationalities, and no doubt some others, were beyond the need of human consideration. "They're waiters and cooks and order men and dishwashers. There's some other kinds, too, but they're mostly waiters."

"Would you say that that old man over there—that fellow with a white beard—was a waiter?"

"Aw, naw! He ain't no waiter. I don't know what he is—pan-handler, maybe. They wouldn't have the likes of him. It's these other fellows that are waiters, these young ones."

You look, and they are young in a way, lean, with thin lips and narrow chests and sallow faces, a little shabby, all of them, and each has a roll of something wrapped up in a newspaper or a brown paper and tucked under his arm—an apron, maybe.

You begin speculating for yourself, and, with the aid of your friend to supply occasional points, you piece the whole thing together. This is really a very great, hard, cold city, and these men are creatures at the bottom of the ladder, temporarily, anyhow. And these columns of ads in the successful morning papers attract them as a chance. And they come here thus early in the cold in order to get a good start on a given job before any one else can get ahead of them. First come, first served.

And while you are waiting, speculating, another creature edges near you. He is not quite so prosperous looking as the last one you talked to; he seems thinner, more emaciated.

"Take a look at that, boss," he says, opening his palm and shoving something bright toward you. It looks like gold.

"No," you answer nervously. (You have been held up before.) "No, I don't want to look at it."

"Take a look at it," he insists.

"No," you retort irritably, but you do it in a half-hearted, objecting way and see that it is a gold ring with an initial carved in the seal plate.

He closes his thin hand and puts it back in his pocket.

He is inclined to go away, and then another idea strikes him.

"Are you lookin' fer a job?" he asks.

"No."

"Ain't you a cook?"

"No."

"Gee! I thought you was some swell chef—they come here now and then."

It is a doubtful compliment but better than nothing. You soften a little.

"I'm a waiter," he confides, now that he has your momentary interest. "I am, I mean, when I'm in good health. I'm run down some now. The best I can get is dishwashing now. But I am a waiter, and I've been an order clerk. There's nothin' much to say of this bunch, though. They all work for the cheap joints. Saturday nights they gits drunk mostly, and if they're not there on the dot Sunday they're gone. The boss gits a new one. Then they come here Sunday night or Monday."

You are inclined to agree that this description fits in pretty well with your observation of a number of them, but what of these others who look like family men, who look worried and harried?

"Sure, there's lots others," prompts your adviser. "There's three columns every day callin' for painters. There's a column most every day of printers. People paints houses all the year round. There's general help wanted. There's carpenters. It gits some. Cooks and waiters and dishwashers in the big pull, though."

You have been wondering if this is really true, but

it sounds plausible enough. These men are obviously, in a great many cases, cooks and waiters. Their search calls for an early start, for the restaurants and hotels usually keep open all night. It may be.

And all the time you have been wondering why the papers do not come. It seems a shame that these men should have to stand here so long. There's a great crowd now, between two and three hundred. A policeman is tramping up and down, keeping an open passageway. He is not in any friendly mood.

"Stand back," he orders angrily. "I'm tellin' ye fer the last time, now!"

A great passageway opens.

Now of a sudden comes a boy running with a great bundle of the most successful morning paper, a most staggering load. Actually the crowd looks as though it would seize him and tear his bundle away from him. but instead it only closes in quickly behind. When he reaches the Irish woman's stand there is a great struggling, grabbing circle formed. "The ——," is the cry. "Gimme a ——," and for the space of a half dozen minutes a thriving, exciting business is done in morning papers. Then these men run with their papers like dogs run with a bone. They hurry, each to some neighboring light, and glance up and down the columns. Sometimes they mark something, and then you see them hurry on again. They have picked their prospect.

It is a pitiful spectacle from one point of view, a decidedly grim one from another. Your dishwasher (or ex-waiter) confides that most of these positions, apart from tips, pay only five dollars a week and board. And

THE MEN IN THE DARK 227

he admits that the board is vile. While you are talking
you recognize some gentlemanly newspaper man, well-
salaried, taking his belated way home. What a contrast!
What a far cry!

"And say," says your dishwasher friend, "I thought
I'd git a job to-night. I thought somebody'd buy this
ring. It'll bring $1.75 in the pawnshop in the mornin'.
I ain't got carfare or I wouldn't mention it. I usually
soaks it early in the week and gits it out Saturday. I'll
soak it to-morrow, and git another chance to-morrow
night."

What a story! What a predicament!

You go down in your pocket and produce a quarter.
You buy him a paper. "On your way," you say cheerily
—but the misery! The depths! To think that any
one of us should come to this!

As he goes you watch the others going, and then the
silence settles down and the night. There is no sense
of traffic here now, no great need of light. The old Irish
woman sinks to the dismal task of waiting, for morning,
I presume. Now and then some passing pedestrian will
buy a paper, but not often. But these others—they have
gone in the direction of the four winds of heaven; they
are applying at the shabby doors of restaurants, in
Brooklyn, Manhattan, the Bronx, Hoboken, Staten
Island; they are sitting on stoops, holding their own at
shop doors. They have the right to ask first, the right
to be first, because they are first—noble privilege.

And you and I—well, we turn in our dreams and
rest. The great world wags on. Our allotted portion
is not this. We are not of these men in the dark.

THE MEN IN THE STORM

Iᴛ is a winter evening. Already, at four o'clock, the
somber hues of night are over all. A heavy snow is
falling, a fine, picking, whipping snow, borne forward
by a swift wind in long, thin lines. The street is bedded
with it, six inches of cold, soft carpet, churned brown by
the crush of teams and the feet of men. Along the
Bowery men slouch through it with collars up and hats
pulled over their ears.

Before a dirty, four-story building gathers a crowd of
men. It begins with the approach of two or three, who
hang about the closed wooden door and beat their feet
to keep them warm. They make no effort to go in, but
shift ruefully about, digging their hands deep in their
pockets and leering at the crowd and the increasing
lamps. There are old men with grizzled beards and
sunken eyes; men who are comparatively young but
shrunken by disease; men who are middle-aged.

With the growth of the crowd about the door comes
a murmur. It is not conversation, but a running comment directed at any one. It contains oaths and slang
phrases.

"I wisht they'd hurry up."

"Look at the cop watchin'."

"Maybe it ain't winter, nuther."

"I wisht I was with Peary."

Now a sharper lash of wind cuts down, and they

huddle closer. There is no anger, no threatening words. It is all sullen endurance, unlightened by either wit or good fellowship.

An automobile goes jingling by with some reclining figure in it. One of the members nearest the door sees it.

"Look at the bloke ridin'!"

"He ain't so cold."

"Eh! eh! eh!" yells another, the automobile having long since passed out of hearing.

Little by little the night creeps on. Along the walk a crowd hurries on its way home. Still the men hang around the door, unwavering.

"Ain't they ever goin' to open up?" queries a hoarse voice suggestively.

This seems to renew general interest in the closed door, and many gaze in that direction. They look at it as dumb brutes look, as dogs paw and whine and study the knob. They shift and blink and mutter, now a curse, now a comment. Still they wait, and still the snow whirls and cuts them.

A glimmer appears through the transom overhead, where some one is lighting the light. It sends a thrill of possibility through the watchers. On the old hats and peaked shoulders snow is piling. It gathers in little heaps and curves, and no one brushes it off. In the center of the crowd the warmth and steam melt it and water trickles off hat-rims and down noses, which the owners cannot reach to scratch. On the outer rim the piles remain unmelted. Those who cannot get in the center, lower their heads to the weather and bend their forms.

At last the bars grate inside, and the crowd pricks up its ears. There is some one who calls: "Slow up there, now!" and then the door opens. It is push and jam for a minute, with grim, beast silence to prove its quality, and then the crowd lessens. It melts inward, like logs floating, and disappears. There are wet hats and shoulders, a cold, shrunken, disgruntled mass pouring in between bleak walls. It is just six o'clock, and there is supper in every hurrying pedestrian's face.

"Do you sell anything to eat here?" one questions of the grizzled old carpet-slippers who opens the door.

"No, nuthin but beds."

The waiting throng had been housed for the night.

THE MEN IN THE SNOW

WINTER days in a great city bring some peculiar sights. If it snows, the streets are at once a slushy mess, and the transaction of business is, to a certain extent, a hardship. In its first flakes it is picturesque; the air is filled with flying feathers and the sky lowery with somber clouds. Later comes the slush and dirt, and not infrequently bitter cold. The city rings with the grind and squeak of cold-bitten vehicles, and men and women, the vast tide of humanity which fills its streets, hurry to and fro so as to be through with the work or need that keeps them out of doors.

In certain sections of the city at a period like this may be found groups of men who are constituted by nature and conditions to be an integral part of every storm. They are like the gulls that follow the schools of fish at sea. Poverty is the bond which makes them kin and gives them, after a fashion, a class distinction. They are not only always poor in body, but poor in mind also, and as for earthly belongings, of course they have not any.

These men, like the gulls and their fish, pick a little something from the storm. They follow the fortunes of the contractors who make arrangements with the city for the removal of the snow, and about the wagon-barns where the implements of snow removal are kept, and where daily cards of employment are issued they may

231

be seen waiting by hundreds, and not at such hours and
under such conditions as are at all pleasant to contemplate, either. In the early hours of the morning, when
the work of the day is first being doled out, they may be
seen, cold, overcoatless, often with bare hands and necks,
no collar, or, if so, only a rag of a thing, and hats too
battered and timeworn to be honestly dignified by the
name of hat at all.

The city usually pays at the rate of two dollars a day
for what shoveling these men can do. They are not
wanted even at that rate by the contractors, for stray,
healthy laborers are usually preferred; but the pressure
under which the contractors are put by the city and the
public makes a showing necessary. So thousands are
admitted to temporary labor who would not otherwise
be considered, and these are they.

So in this cold, raw, strenuous weather they stand like
so many sheep waiting at the entrance to a fold. There
is no particular zeal in this effort which they are making
to live. Hunger for life they have, but it is a rundown
hunger, dispirited by lack of encouragement. They have
been kicked and pushed about the world in an effort to
live until, as a rule, they are comparatively heartbroken
and courage-broken. This storm, which spells comfort
and indoor seclusion and amusement for many, spells a
rough opportunity for them—a gutter crust, to be sure,
but a crust.

And so they are here early in the morning, in the
dark. They stand in a long file outside the contractors'
stable door, waiting for that consideration which his
present need may show. A man at a little glass window

cut in a door receives them. He is a hearty, material,
practical soul who has very little to suggest in the way
of mentality but much in the spirit of acquisitiveness.
He is not interested in the condition of the individuals
before him. It does not concern him that in most cases
this is a last despairing grasp at a straw. Will this
fellow work? Will he be satisfied to take $1.75 in place
of the $2.00 which the city pays? He does not ask them
that so clearly; it is done in another way.

"Got a shovel?"

"No, sir."

"Well, it'll cost you a quarter to get one."

"I ain't got no quarter."

"Well, that's all right. We'll take it out o' your
pay."

Not for to-day only, mind you, but for every day
in which work is done, the quarter comes out for the
shovel. It is suggested in some sections that the shovel
is sometimes stolen, but there are gang foremen, and no
money is paid without a foreman's O. K., and he is
responsible for the shovels. . . . Hence——

But these men are a bit of dramatic color in the city's
life, whatever their sufferings. To see them following
in droves through the bitter winter streets the great
wagons which haul the snow away is fascinating, at times
pitiful. I have seen old men with white beards and
uncut snowy hair shoveling snow into a truck. I have
seen lean, unfed strips of boys without overcoats and
with long, lean, red hands protruding from undersized
coat sleeves, doing the same thing. I have seen anæmic

benchers and consumptives following along illy clad
but shoveling weakly in the snow and cold.

It is a sad mix-up at best, this business of living.
Fortune deals so haphazardly at birth and at death
that it is hard to criticize. It so indifferently smashes
the dreams of kings and beggars, dealing the golden
sequins to the sleeping man, taking from the earnest
plodder the little which he has gained, that one becomes,
at last, confused. It is easy for many to criticize, for
one reason and another, and justly mayhap, but at the
same time it is so easy to see how it all may have come
about. Wit has not always been present, but sickness,
a perverted moral point of view, an error in honesty, and
the climbing of years is over; the struggling toad has
fallen back into the well. There is now nothing but
struggle and crumb-picking at the bottom. And these
are they.

And so these storms, like the bread-line, like the
Bowery Lodging, offer them something; not much. A
few days, and the snow will be over. A few days, and
the sun of a warm day will end all opportunity for work.
They will go back again into the gloomy adventuring
whence they emerged. Only now they are visible collectively, here in the cold and the snow, shoveling.

I like to think of them best and worst, though, as I
have seen them time and time again waiting outside
the wagon barns at night, the labor of the day over.
It is something even to be a "down-and-out" and stand
waiting for a pittance which one has really earned. You
can see something of the satisfaction of this even in this
gloomy line. In the early dark of a winter evening,

the street's lamps lighted, these men are shuffling their feet to keep warm. They are waiting to be paid, as they are at the end of each work day, but in their hearts is a faint response to the thought of gain—one dollar and seventy-five cents for the long day in the cold. The quarter is yielded gladly. The contractor finds a fat profit in the many quarters he can so easily garner. But these? To them it is a satisfaction to get the wherewithal to face another day. It is something to have the money wherewith to obtain a lodging and a meal for a night. That one-seventy-five—how really large it must look, like fifty or a hundred or a thousand to some. Satisfactions and joys are all so relative. But they have really earned one dollar and seventy-five cents and can hurry away to that marvelous table of satisfaction which one dollar and seventy-five cents will provide.

THE FRESHNESS OF THE UNIVERSE

THE freshness of the world's original forces is one of the wonders which binds me in perpetual fascination. My own strength is a little thing. I am sometimes sick and sometimes well; some days I am bounding with enthusiastic life, at other times I am drooping with weariness and ill feeling. But these things, the great currents of original power which make the world, are fresh and forever renewing themselves.

Every morning I rise from my sleep restored and go out of doors, and there they are. At the foot of my garden is a river which has been running all night long, a swift and never-resting stream. It has been running so every day and every night for centuries and centuries—and thousands of centuries, for all I know— and yet here it runs. People have come and gone; nations have risen and fallen; all sorts of puny strengths have had their day and have perished; but this thing has never weakened nor modified itself nor changed,— at least not very much. Its life is so long and so strong.

And another thing that strikes me is the force and persistency of the winds. How sweet they are, how refreshing to the wearied body! I rise with sluggishness, and a sense of disgust with the world, mayhap, and yet here are the winds, fresh as in the beginning, to run me through and cool my face and hands and fill my breast with pure air and make me think the world is good again.

236

I step out of my doorway, and here they are, blowing across the garden, shaking the leaves of the trees, rustling in the grass, fluttering at my coat-sleeves and my hair; and I am no whit the wiser as to what they are. Only I know that they are old, old, and yet as strong and invigorating as they ever were, and will be when my little strength is wasted and I am no more.

And here is the sun, bright, golden thing of the sky, which I may not even look at directly but which makes my day just the same. It is so invigorating, so healing, so beautiful. I know it is a commonplace, the thing that must have been before I could be, and yet it is so novel and fresh and new, even now. I rise, and this old sunlight is the newest thing in the world. Beside this day, which it makes, all things are old—my little house, which after all has stood only a few years; my possessions, dusty with standing a little while, and fading; myself, who am less young and strong by a day, getting older. And yet here it is, new after a million years— and a billion years, for aught I know—pouring this golden flood into my garden and making it what I wish it to be, new. The wonder of this force is appealing to me. It touches the innermost strangeness of my being.

And then there is the earth upon which I stand, strange chemic dust, here covered with grass but elsewhere covered with trees and flowers and hard habitations of men, yielding its perennial toll of beauty. We cannot understand the ground, but its newness, the perennial force with which it produces our food and beauty, this is so patent to all. I look at the ground beneath my feet, and lo, the agedness of it does not

occur to me, only its freshness. The good ground!
The new earth! This thing which is old, old—old as
Time itself—must always have been and must always
be. Where was it before it was here? What stars did
it make, and moons? What ancient lives have trod
this earth, this ground beneath my feet, and now make
it? And yet how comes it that I who am so young find
it so new to me and myself old as compared with its
tremendous age! That is the wonder of this original
force to me.

And in my yard are trees and little things such as
vines and stone walls, which, for all their newness and
briefness, have so much more enduring power than have
I. This tree near my door is fully a hundred years
old, and yet it will be young, comparatively speaking,
and strong, when I am no longer in existence. Its
trunk is straight, its head is high, and here am I who,
looking upon it now as old, will soon be older in spirit,
unable to bear the too-heavy burden of a short existence
and tottering wearily about when it will still be strong
and straight, good for another life the length of mine—
a strange contrast of forces. That is but one of the
wonders of the forces of life: their persistence.

Yet it is this morning waking that impresses the
marvel of their greatness upon me. It is this new day,
this new-old river, this new-old tree, the new earth, so
old and yet so new, which point the frailty of my physical
and mental existence and make me wonder what the
riddle of the universe may be.

THE CRADLE OF TEARS

THERE is a cradle within the door of one of the great institutions of New York before which a constant recurring tragedy is being enacted. It is a plain cradle, quite simply draped in white, but with such a look of cozy comfort about it that one would scarcely suspect it to be a cradle of sorrow.

A little white bed, with a neatly turned-back coverlet, is made up within it. A long strip of white muslin, tied in a tasteful bow at the top, drapes its rounded sides. About it, but within the precincts of warmth and comfort of which it is a part, spreads a chamber of silence—a quiet, small, plainly furnished room, the appearance of which emphasizes the peculiarity of the cradle itself.

If the mind were not familiar with the details with which it is so startlingly associated, the question would naturally arise as to what it was doing there, why it should be standing there alone. No one seems to be watching it. It has not the slightest appearance of usefulness. And yet there it stands day after day, and year after year, a ready-prepared cradle, and no infant to live in it.

And yet this cradle is the most useful, and, in a way, the most inhabited cradle in the world. Day after day and year after year it is a recipient of more small wayfaring souls than any other cradle in the world. In it the real children of sorrow are placed, and over it more tears are shed than if it were an open grave.

It is a place where annually twelve hundred found-lings are placed, many of them by mothers who are too helpless or too unfortunately environed to be further able to care for their children; and the misery which compels it makes of the little open crib a cradle of tears.

The interest of this cradle is that it has been the silent witness of more truly heartbreaking scenes than any other cradle since the world began. For nearly sixty years it has stood where it does to-day, ready-draped, open, while almost as many thousand mothers have stolen shamefacedly in and after looking hopelessly about have laid their helpless offspring within its depths.

For sixty years, winter and summer, in the bitterest cold and the most stifling heat, it has seen them come, the poor, the rich, the humble, the proud, the beautiful, the homely; and one by one they have laid their children down and brooded over them, wondering if it were possible for human love to make so great a sacrifice and yet not die.

And then, when the child has been actually sacrificed, when by the simple act of releasing their hold upon it and turning away, they have allowed it to pass out from their loving tenderness into the world unknown, this silent cradle has seen them smite their hands in anguish and yield to such voiceless tempests of grief as only those know who have loved much and lost all.

The circumstances under which this peculiar charity comes to be a part of the life of the great metropolis need not be rehearsed here. The heartlessness of men, the frailty of women, the brutality of all those who sit in judgment in spite of the fact that they do not wish to be judged themselves, is so old and so commonplace that its repetition is almost wearisome.

Still, the tragedy repeats itself, and year after year and day after day the unlocked door is opened and dethroned virtue enters—the victim of ignorance and passion and affection—and a child is robbed of a home.

I think there is a significant though concealed thought here, for nature in thus repeating a fact day after day and year after year raises a significant question. We are so dull. Sometimes it requires ten thousand or ten million repetitions to make us understand. "Here is a condition. What will you do about it? Here is a condition. What will you do about it? Here is a condition. What will you do about it?" That is the question each tragedy propounds, and finally we wake and listen. Then slowly some better way is discovered, some theory developed. We find often that there is an answer to some questions, at least if we have to remake ourselves, society, the face of the world, to get it.

WHENCE THE SONG

ALONG Broadway in the height of the theatrical season, but more particularly in that laggard time from June to September, when the great city is given over to those who may not travel, and to actors seeking engagements, there is ever to be seen a certain representative figure, now one individual and now another, of a world so singular that it might well engage the pen of a Balzac or that of a Cervantes. I have in mind an individual whose high hat and smooth Prince Albert coat are still a delicious presence. In his coat lapel is a ruddy boutonnière, in his hand a novel walking-stick. His vest is of a gorgeous and affluent pattern, his shoes shiny-new and topped with pearl-gray spats. With dignity he carries his body and his chin. He is the cynosure of many eyes, the envy of all men, and he knows it. He is the successful author of the latest popular song.

Along Broadway, from Union to Greeley Squares, any fair day during the period of his artistic elevation, he is to be seen. Past the rich shops and splendid theaters he betakes himself with leisurely grace. In Thirtieth Street he may turn for a few moments, but it is only to say good-morning to his publishers. In Twenty-eighth Street, where range the host of those who rival his successful house, he stops to talk with lounging actors and ballad singers. Well-known variety stars nod to him familiarly. Women whose sole claim to distinction lies in their knack of singing a song, smile in greeting as he passes. Occasionally there comes a figure of a needy ballad-monger, trudging from publisher to publisher with an unavailable manuscript, who turns upon him, in passing, the glint of an envious glance. To these he is an important figure, satisfied as much with their envy as with their praise, for is not this also his due, the reward of all who have triumphed?

I have in mind another figure, equally singular: a rouged and powdered little maiden, rich in feathers and ornaments of the latest vogue; gloved in blue and shod in yellow; pretty, self-assured, daring, and even bold. There has gone here all the traditional maidenly reserve you would expect to find in one so young and pleasing, and yet she is not evil. The daughter of a Chicago butcher, you knew her when she first came to the city—a shabby, wondering little thing, clerk to a music publisher transferring his business east, and all eyes for the marvels of city life.

Gradually the scenes and superlatives of elegance, those showy men and women coming daily to secure or sell songs, have aroused her longings and ambitions. Why may not she sing, why not she be a theatrical celebrity? She will. The world shall not keep her down. That elusive and almost imaginary company known as *they*, whose hands are ever against the young, shall not hold her back.

Behold, for a time, then, she has gone; and now, elegant, jingling with silver ornaments, hale and merry from good living, she has returned. To-day she is playing at one of the foremost vaudeville houses. To-morrow she leaves for Pittsburgh. Her one object is still a salary of five hundred or a thousand a week and a three-sheet litho of herself in every window and upon every billboard.

"I'm all right now," she will tell you gleefully. "I'm way ahead of the knockers. They can't keep me down. You ought to have seen the reception I got in Pittsburgh. Say, it was the biggest yet."

Blessed be Pittsburgh, which has honored one who has struggled so hard, and you say so.

"Are you here for long?"

"Only this week. Come up and see my turn. Hey, cabbie!"

A passing cabman turns in close to the walk with considerable alacrity.

"Take me to Keith's. So long. Come up and see my turn to-night."

This is the woman singer, the complement of the male of the same art, the couple who make for the acceptance and spread of the popular song as well as the fame of its author. They sing them in every part of the country, and here in New York, returned from a long season on the road, they form a very important portion of this song-writing, song-singing world. They and the authors and the successful publishers—but we may simplify by yet another picture.

In Twenty-seventh or Twenty-eighth Street, or anywhere along Broadway from Madison to Greeley Squares, are the parlors of a score of publishers, gentlemen who coördinate this divided world for song publishing purposes. There is an office and a reception-room; a music-chamber, where songs are tried, and a stock room. Perhaps, in the case of the larger publishers, the music-rooms are two or three, but the air of each is much the same. Rugs, divans, imitation palms make this publishing house more bower than office. Three or four pianos give to each chamber a parlor-like appearance. The walls are hung with the photos of celebrities, neatly framed, celebrities of the kind described. In the private music-rooms, rocking-chairs. A boy or two waits to bring *professional copies* at a word. A salaried pianist or two wait to run over pieces which the singer may desire to hear. Arrangers wait to make orchestrations or take down newly schemed out melodies which the popular composer himself cannot play. He has evolved the melody by a process of whistling and must have its fleeting beauty registered before it escapes him forever. Hence the salaried arranger.

Into these parlors then, come the mixed company of this distinctive world: authors who have or have not succeeded, variety artists who have some word from touring fellows or know the firm, masters of small bands throughout the city or the country, of which the name is legion, orchestra-leaders of Bowery theaters and up-town variety halls, and singers.

"You haven't got a song that will do for a tenor, have you?"

The inquirer is a little, stout, ruddy-faced Irish boy from the gas-house district. His common clothes are not out of the ordinary here, but they mark him as possibly a non-professional seeking free copies.

"Sure, let me see. For what do you want it?"

"Well, I'm from the Arcadia Pleasure Club. We're

going to give a little entertainment next Wednesday and we want some songs.''

"I think I've got just the thing you want. Wait till I call the boy. Harry! Bring me some professional copies of ballads.''

The youth is probably a representative of one of the many Tammany pleasure organizations, the members of which are known for their propensity to gather about east and west side corners at night and sing. One or two famous songs are known to have secured their start by the airing given them in this fashion on the street corners of the great city.

Upon his heels treads a lady whose ruffled sedateness marks her as one unfamiliar with this half-musical, half-theatrical atmosphere.

"I have a song I would like to have you try over, if you care to.''

The attending publisher hesitates before even extending a form of reception.

"What sort of a song is it?''

"Well, I don't exactly know. I guess you'd call it a sentimental ballad. If you'd hear it I think you might——''

"We are so over-stocked with songs now, Madam, that I don't believe there's much use in our hearing it. Could you come in next Friday? We'll have more leisure then and can give you more attention.''

The lady looks the failure she has scored, but retreats, leaving the ground clear for the chance arrival of the real author, the individual whose position is attested by one hit or mayhap many. His due is that deference

which all publishers, if not the public, feel called upon
to render, even if at the time he may have no reigning
success.

"Hello, Frank, how are you? What's new?"

The author, cane in hand, may know of nothing in
particular.

"Sit down. How are things with you, anyhow?"

"Oh, so-so."

"That new song of yours will be out Friday. We have
a rush order on it."

"Is that so?"

"Yes, and I've got good news for you. Windom
going to sing it next year with the minstrels. He was
in here the other day and thought it was great."

"Well, that's good."

"That song's going to go, all right. You haven't got
any others, have you?"

"No, but I've got a tune. Would you mind having
one of the boys take it down for me?"

"Surest thing you know. Here, Harry! Call Hatcher."

Now comes the pianist and arranger, and a hearing and
jotting down of the new melody in a private room. The
favored author may have piano and pianist for an indefinite period any time. Lunch with the publishers awaits
him if he remains until noon. His song, when ready, is
heard with attention. The details which make for its
publication are rushed. His royalties are paid with
that rare smile which accompanies the payment of anything to one who earns money for another. He is to be
petted, conciliated, handled with gloves.

At his heels, perhaps, another author, equally successful, maybe, but almost intolerable because of certain marked eccentricities of life and clothing. He is a negro, small, slangy, strong in his cups, but able to write a good song, occasionally a truly pathetic ballad.

"Say, where's that gem o' mine?"

"What?"

"That effusion."

"What are you talking about?"

"That audience-killer—that there thing that's goin' to sweep the country like wildfire—that there song."

Much laughter and apology.

"It will be here Friday, Gussie."

"Thought it was to be here last Monday?"

"So it was, but the printers didn't get it done. You know how those things are, Gussie."

"I know. Gimme twenty-five dollars."

"Sure. But what are you going to do with it?"

"Never you mind. Gimme twenty-five bones. To-morrow's rent day up my way."

Twenty-five is given as if it were all a splendid joke. Gussie is a bad negro, one day radiant in bombastic clothing, the next wretched from dissipation and neglect. He has no royalty coming to him, really. That is, he never accepts royalty. All his songs are sold outright. But these have earned the house so much that if he were to demand royalties the sum to be paid would beggar anything he has ever troubled to ask for.

"I wouldn't take no royalty," he announces at one time, with a bombastic and yet mellow negro emphasis, which is always amusing. "Doan want it. Too much trouble. All I want is money when I needs it and wants it.''

Seeing that nearly every song that he writes is successful, this is a most equitable arrangement. He could have several thousand instead of a few hundred, but being shiftless he does not care. Ready money is the thing with him, twenty-five or fifty when he needs it.

And then those ''peerless singers of popular ballads,'' as their programs announce them, men and women whose pictures you will see upon every song-sheet, their physiognomy underscored with their own ''Yours Sincerely'' in their own handwriting. Every day they are here, arriving and departing, carrying the latest songs to all parts of the land. These are the individuals who in their own estimation ''make'' the songs the successes they are. In all justice, they have some claim to the distinction. One such, raising his or her voice nightly in a melodic interpretation of a new ballad, may, if the music be sufficiently catchy, bring it so thoroughly to the public ear as to cause it to begin to sell. These individuals are not unaware of their services in the matter, nor slow to voice their claims. In flocks and droves they come, whenever good fortune brings ''the company'' to New York or the end of the season causes them to return, to tell of their success and pick new songs for the ensuing season. Also to collect certain pre-arranged bonuses. Also to gather news and dispense it. Then, indeed, is the day of the publisher's volubility and grace. These gentlemen and ladies must be attended to with that deference which is the right of the successful. The ladies must be praised and cajoled.

"Did you hear about the hit I made with 'Sweet Kitty Leary' in Kansas City? I knocked 'em cold. Say, it was the biggest thing on the bill."

The publisher may not have heard of it. The song, for all the uproarious success depicted, may not have sold an extra copy, and yet this is not for him to say. Has the lady a good voice? Is she with a good company? He may so ingratiate himself that she will yet sing one of his newer and as yet unheard of compositions into popularity.

"Was it? Well, I'm glad to hear it. You have the voice for that sort of a song, you know, Marie. I've got something new, though, that will just suit you—oh, a dandy. It's by Harry Welch."

For all this flood of geniality the singer may only smile indifferently. Secretly her hand is against all publishers. They are out for themselves. Successful singers must mind their P's and Q's. Payment is the word, some arrangement by which she shall receive a stated sum per week for singing a song. The honeyed phrases are well enough for beginners, but we who have succeeded need something more.

"Let me show you something new. I've got a song here that is fine. Come right into the music-room. Charlie, get a copy of 'She May Have Seen Better Days.' I want you to play it over for Miss Yaeger."

The boy departs and returns. In the exclusive music-room sits the singer, critically listening while the song is played.

"Isn't that a pretty chorus?"

"Well, yes, I rather like that."

"That will suit your voice exactly. Don't ever doubt it. I think that's one of the best songs we have published in years."

"Have you the orchestration?"

"Sure; I'll get you that."

Somehow, however, the effect has not been satisfactory. The singer has not enthused. He must try other songs and give her the orchestrations of many. Perhaps, out of all, she will sing one. That is the chance of the work.

As for her point of view, she may object to the quality of anything except for that which she is paid. It is for the publisher to see whether she is worth subsidizing or not. If not, perhaps another house will see her merits in a different light. Yet she takes the songs and orchestrations along. And the publisher turning, as she goes, announces, "Gee, there's a cold proposition for you. Get her to sing anything for you for nothing?—Nix. Not her. Cash or no song." And he thumbs his fingers after the fashion of one who pays out money.

Your male singer is often a bird of the same fine feather. If you wish to see the ideal of dressiness as exemplified by the gentlemen of the road, see these individuals arrive at the offices of the publishers. The radiance of half-hose and neckties is not outdone by the sprightliness of the suit pattern or the glint of the stone in the shirt-front. Fresh from Chicago or Buffalo they arrive, rich

in self-opinion fostered by rural praise, perhaps possessed of a new droll story, always loaded with the details of the hit they made.

"Well, well! You should have seen how that song
went in Baltimore. I never saw anything like it. Why,
it's the hit of the season!"

New songs are forthcoming, a new batch delivered
for his service next year.

Is he absolutely sure of the estimation in which the
house holds his services? You will hear a sequel to this,
not this day perhaps but a week or a month later, during
his idle summer in New York.

"You haven't twenty-five handy you could let me
have, have you, Pat? I'm a little short to-day."

Into the publisher's eye steals the light of wisdom and
decision. Is this individual worth it? Will he do the
songs of the house twenty-five dollars' worth of good
next season? Blessed be fate if there is a partner to
consult. He will have time to reflect.

"Well, George, I haven't it right here in the drawer,
but I can get it for you. I always like to consult my
partner about these things, you know. Can you wait
until this afternoon?"

Of course the applicant can wait, and between whiles
are conferences and decisions. All things considered,
it may be advisable to do it.

"We will get twenty-five out of him, any way. He's
got a fine tenor voice. You never can tell what he
might do."

So a pleasant smile and the money may be waiting

when he returns. Or, he may be put off, with excuses and apologies. It all depends.

There are cases, however, where not even so much delay can be risked, where a hearty "sure" *must* be given. This is to that lord of the stage whose fame as a singer is announced by every minstrel billboard as "the renowned baritone, Mr. Calvin Johnson," or some such. For him the glad hand and the ready check, and he is to be petted, flattered, taken to lunch, dinner, a box theater party—anything—everything, really. And then, there is that less important one who has over-measured his importance. For him the solemn countenance and the suave excuse, at an hour when his need is greatest. Lastly, there is the sub-strata applicant in tawdry, make-believe clothes, whose want peeps out of every seam and pocket. His day has never been as yet, or mayhap was, and is over. He has a pinched face, a livid hunger, a forlorn appearance. Shall he be given anything? Never. He is not worth it. He is a "dead one." Is it not enough if the publisher looks after those of whose ability he is absolutely sure. Certainly. Therefore this one must slop the streets in old shoes and thin clothing, waiting. And he may never obtain a dime from any publisher.

Out of such grim situations, however, occasionally springs a success. These "down and out" individuals do not always understand why fate should be against them, why they should be down, and are not willing to cease trying.

"I'll write a song yet, you bet," is the dogged, grim decision. "I'll get up, you bet."

Once in a while the threat is made good, some mood

allowing. Strolling along the by-streets, ignored and self-commiserating, the mood seizes them. Words bubble up and a melody, some crude commentary on the contrasts, the losses or the hopes of life, rhyming, swinging as they come, straight from the heart. Now it is for pencil and paper, quick. Any old scrap will do—the edge of a newspaper, the back of an envelope, the edge of a cuff. Written so, the words are safe and the melody can be whistled until some one will take it down. And so, occasionally, is born—has been often—the great success, the land-sweeping melody, selling by the hundreds of thousands and netting the author a thousand a month for a year or more.

Then, for him, the glory of the one who is at last successful. Was he commonplace, hungry, envious, wretchedly clothed before? Well, now, see! And do not talk to him of other authors who once struck it, had their little day and went down again, never to rise. He is not of them—not like them. For him, now, the sunlight and the bright places. No clothing too showy or too expensive, no jewelry too rare. Broadway is the place for him, the fine cafés and rich hotel lobbies. What about those other people who looked down on him once? Ha! they scorned him, did they? They sneered, eh? Would not give him a cent, eh? Let them come and look now! Let them stare in envy. Let them make way. He is a great man at last and the whole world knows it. The whole country is making acclaim over that which he has done.

For the time being, then, this little center of song-writing and publishing is for him the all-inclusive of life's importance. From the street organs at every corner is being ground the *one* melody, so expressive of his personality, into the ears of all men. In the vaudeville houses and cheaper concert halls men and women are singing it nightly to uproarious applause. Parodies are made and catch-phrases coined, all speaking of his work. Newsboys whistle and older men pipe its peculiar notes. Out of open windows falls the distinguished melody, accompanied by voices both new and strange. All men seem to recognize that which he has done, and for the time being compliment his presence and his personality.

Then the wane.

Of all the tragedies, this is perhaps the bitterest, because of the long-drawn memory of the thing. Organs continue to play it, but the sale ceases. Quarter after quarter, the royalties are less, until at last a few dollars per month will measure them completely. Meanwhile his publishers ask for other songs. One he writes, and then another, and yet another, vainly endeavoring to duplicate that original note which made for his splendid success the year before. But it will not come. And, in the meanwhile, other song-writers displace him for the time being in the public eye. His publishers have a new hit, but it is not his. A new author is being bowed to and taken out to dinner. But he is not that author. A new tile-crowned celebrity is strolling up his favorite Broadway path. At last, after a dozen attempts and failures, there is no hurry to publish his songs. If the period of failure is too long extended he may even be neglected. More and more, celebrities crowd in between him and that delightful period when he was greatest. At last,

chagrined by the contrast of things, he changes his publishers, changes his haunts and, bitterest of all, his style
of living. Soon it is the old grind again, and then, if
thoughtless spending has been his failing, shabby clothing and want. You may see the doubles of these in any
publisher's sanctum at any time, the sarcastically re-
ferred-to *has been.*

Here, also, the disengaged ballad singer, "peerless
tenor" of some last year's company, suffering a period
of misfortune. He is down on his luck in everything but
appearances, last year's gorgeousness still surviving in
a modified and sedate form. He is a singer of songs,
now, for the publishers, by toleration. His one loung-
ing-place in all New York where he is welcome and not
looked at askance is the chair they may allow him. Once
a day he makes the rounds of the theatrical agencies;
once, or if fortune favors, twice a day he visits some
cheap eating-house. At night, after a lone stroll through
that fairyland of theaters and gaudy palaces to which,
as he sees it, he properly belongs—Broadway, he returns
to his bed, the carpeted floor of a room in some tolerant
publisher's office, where he sleeps by permission, perhaps,
and not even there, too often.

Oh, the glory of success in this little world in his
eye at this time—how now, in want, it looms large and
essential! Outside, as he stretches himself, may even
now be heard the murmur of that shiny, joyous rout
of which he was so recently a part. The lights, the
laughter; the songs, the mirth—all are for others. Only
he, only he must linger in shadows, alone.

To-morrow it will come out in words, if you talk with

him. It is in the publisher's office, perhaps, where gaudy ladies are trying songs, or on the street, where others, passing, notice him not but go their way in elegance.

"I had it once, all right," he will tell you. "I had my handful. You bet I'll get it next year."

Is it of money he is thinking?

An automobile swings past and some fine lady, looking out, wakes to bitterness his sense of need.

"New York's tough without the coin, isn't it? You never get a glance when you're out of the game. I spend too easy, that's what's the matter with me. But I'll get back, you bet. Next time I'll know enough to save. I'll get up again, and next time I'll stay up, see?"

Next year his hopes may be realized again, his dreams come true. If so, be present and witness the glories of radiance after shadow.

"Ah, me boy, back again, you see!"

"So I see. Quite a change since last season."

"Well, I should smile. I was down on my luck then. That won't happen any more. They won't catch me. I've learned a lesson. Say, we had a great season."

Rings and pins attest it. A cravat of marvelous radiance speaks for itself in no uncertain tones. Striped clothes, yellow shoes, a new hat and cane. Ah, the glory, the glory! He is not to be caught any more, "you bet," and yet here is half of his subsistence blooming upon his merry body.

They will catch him, though, him and all in the length of time. One by one they come, old, angular misfortune grabbing them all by the coat-tails. The rich, the proud, the great among them sinking, sinking, staggering backward until they are where he was and deeper, far deeper. I wish I could quote those little notices so common in all our metropolitan dailies, those little perfunctory records which appear from time to time in theatrical and sporting and "song" papers, telling volumes in a line. One day one such singer's voice is failing; another day he has been snatched by disease; one day one radiant author arrives at that white beneficence which is the hospital bed and stretches himself to a final period of suffering; one day a black boat steaming northward along the East River to a barren island and a field of weeds carries the last of all that was so gay, so unthinking, so, after all, childlike of him who was greatest in his world. Weeds and a headboard, salt winds and the cry of seagulls, lone blowings and moanings, and all that light and mirth is buried here.

Here and there in the world are those who are still singing melodies created by those who have gone this unfortunate way, singers of "Two Little Girls in Blue" and "White Wings," "Little Annie Rooney" and "The Picture and the Ring," the authors of "In the Baggage Coach Ahead" and "Trinity Chimes," of "Sweet Marie" and "Eileen"—all are here. There might be recited the successes of a score of years, quaint, pleasing melodies which were sung the land over, which even to-day find an occasional voice and a responsive chord, but of the authors not one but could be found in some field for the outcasts, forgotten. Somehow the world forgets, the peculiar world in which they moved, and the larger one which knew them only by their songs.

It seems strange, really, that so many of them should have come to this. And yet it is true—authors, singers, publishers, even—and yet not more strange is it than that their little feeling, worked into a melody and a set of words, should reach far out over land and water, touching the hearts of the nation. In mansion and hovel, by some blazing furnace of a steel mill, or through the open window of a farmland cottage, is trolled the simple story, written in halting phraseology, tuned as only a popular melody is tuned. All have seen the theater uproarious with those noisy recalls which bring back the sunny singer, harping his one indifferent lay. All have heard the street bands and the organs, the street boys and the street loungers, all expressing a brief melody, snatched from the unknown by some process of the heart. Yes, here it is, wandering the land over like a sweet breath of summer, making for matings and partings, for happiness and pain. That it may not endure is also meet, going back into the soil, as it does, with those who hear it and those who create.

Yet only those who venture here in merry Broadway shall witness the contrast, however. Only they who meet these radiant presences in the flesh will ever know the marvel of the common song.

THE SANDWICH MAN

I WOULD not feel myself justified mentally if at some time or other I had not paused in thought over the picture of the sandwich man. These shabby figures of decayed or broken manhood, how they have always appealed to me. I know what they stand for. I have felt with them. I am sure I have felt beyond them, over and over again, the misery and pathos of their state.

And yet, what a bit of color they add to the life of any city, what a foil to its prosperity, its ease—what a fillip to the imagination of those who have any! Against carriages and autos and showy bursts of enthusiastic life, if there be such, they stand out at times with a vividness which makes the antithesis of their state seem many times more important than it really is. In the face of sickness, health is wonderful. In the face of cold, warmth is immensely significant. In the face of poverty, wealth is truly grandeur and may well strut and stride. And who is so obviously, so notoriously poor as this creature of the two signs, this perambulating pack-horse of an advertisement, this hopeless, decayed creature who, if he have but life enough to walk, will do very well as an invitation to buy.

He is such a biting commentary on life, in one sense, such a coarse, shabby jest in another, that we cannot help but think on him and the conditions which produce him. To send forth an anæmic, hollow-eyed, gaunt-

bodied man carrying an announcement of a good dinner, for instance. Imagine. Or a cure-all. Or a
beauty powder. Or a good suit of clothes. Or a sound
pair of shoes. And these with their toes or their naked
bodies all but exposed to the world. An overcoatless
man advertising a warm overcoat in winter. One from
whom all and even the possibility of joy had fled, dis-
playing a notice of joy in the shape of a sign for a
dance-hall, a theater, a moving picture even. The thick-
witted thoughtlessness of the trade-vulgarian who could
permit this!

But the eyes of them! The cold, red, and often wet
hands! The torn hats with snow on them, the thin
shoes that are soppy with snow or water. Is it not a
biting commentary on the importance of the individual,
as such, that in life he may be used in such a way as
this, in a single short life, as a post upon which to hang
things! And that in the face of all the wealth of the
world—over-production! And that in the face of all the
blather and pother anent the poor, and Christ, and
mercy, and I know not what else!

I once protested to an artist friend who chanced to be
sketching a line of these, carrying signs, that it was a
pity from the individual's point of view, as well as from
that of society itself, that such things must be. But he
did not agree with me. "Not at all," he replied. "They
are mentally and physically pointless, anyhow, aren't
they? They have no imagination, no strength any
more, or they wouldn't be carrying signs. Don't you
think that you are applying your noble emotions to
their state? Why shouldn't they be used? They

haven't your emotions—they haven't any emotions, as
a matter of fact, or very rudimentary ones, and such
as they have they are applying to simpler, cheaper
things than you do yours. Mostly they're dirty and
indifferent, believe me.''

I could not say that I wholly disagreed with him. At
the same time, I could not say that I violently agreed
with him. It is true that life does queer tricks with our
emotions and quondam passions at times. The ones that
are so very powerful this year, where are they next? At
one time we are racked and torn and flayed and blown
by emotions that at another find us quite dead, incapable
of any response. All the nervous ambitions, as well as
the circumstances by which fine emotions and moods are
at one time generated, at another have been entirely
dissipated. Betimes there is nothing left save a disjointed
and weary frame or a wornout brain or nervous system
incapable of emotions and disturbing moods.

Yet, granting the truth of this, what a way to use the
image of the human race, I thought, the image of our old-
time selves! Why degrade the likeness of the thing we
once were and by which once we set so much store and
then expect to raise man's estimate of man? It is written: ''Thou shalt not take the name of the Lord, thy God,
in vain.'' Why take the body of man in so shabby, so
degrading a fashion? Why make a mockery of the
body and mind of the human race, and then expect
something superior of life? We talk of elevating the
human race. Can we use ourselves as signs and then
do that? It is entirely probable, of course, that the
human race cannot be elevated. Very good. But if

we dream of any such thing, what must such a sight
do to the imagination of the world? What conception
of the beauty and sweetness and dignity of life does
it not aid to destroy? What lessons of hardness and
self-preservation and indifference does it not teach?
Does it not glorify health and strength and prosperity
at the expense of every other quality? I think so. To
be strong, to be well, to be prosperous in the face of the
sandwich man—is there anywhere more of an an-
achronism?

I sometimes think that in our general life-classifica-
tions we neglect the individual, the exceptional individual, who is always sure to be everywhere, as readily
at the bottom of society as at the top, as readily sand-
wiched between two glaring signs as anywhere else.
It is quite all right to admit, for argument's sake or our
own peace of mind, that most of these men are dirty and
worn and indifferent, and hence negligible; though it
always seems silly to me to assume that a man is indifferent or negligible when he will pack a sign in the
cold and snow in order to preserve himself. It is so
easy for those of us who are comfortable to assume
that the other man does not care, does not feel. Here
he comes, though, carrying a sign. Why? To be carrying it because it makes no difference to him? Because
he has no emotions? I don't believe it. I could not
believe it. And all the evidence I have personally taken
has been to the contrary, decidedly so.

I remember seeing once, in the rush of the Christmas
trade in New York City a few years ago, a score of these
decidedly shabby and broken brethren carrying signs

for the edification, allurement and information of the
Christmas trade. They were strung out along Sixth
Avenue from Twenty-third to Fourteenth Streets, and
the messages which their billboards carried were various.
I noticed that in the budding gayety of the time these
men alone were practically hopeless, dull and gray. The
air was fairly crackling with the suggestion of interest
and happiness for some. People were hurrying hither
and thither, eager about their purchases. There were
great van-loads of toys and fineries constantly being
moved and transferred. Life seemed to say: ''This is
the season of gifts and affection,'' but it obviously meant
nothing to these men. I took a five-dollar bill and had
it changed into half-dollars. I stopped before the first
old wizened loiterer I met, his sign hanging like a cross
from his gaunt shoulder, and before his unsuspecting
eyes lifted the half-dollar. Who could be offering him
a half-dollar? his eyes seemed indifferently to ask at
first. Then a perfect eagle's gleam flashed into them,
old and dull as they were, and a claw-like hand reached
for it. No thanks, no acknowledgment, no polite recognition—just grim realization that money, a whole
half-dollar, was being given, and a physical, wholly
animal determination to get it. What possibilities that
half-dollar seemed to hold to that indifferent, unimag-
inative mind at that moment! What it suggested, apparently, of possible comfort! Why? Because there was
no imagination there? because life meant nothing? Not
in that case, surely. A whole epic of failure and desire
was written in that gleam—and we speak of them as
emotionless.

I went further with my half-dollars. I learned what a half-dollar means to a man in a sandwich sign in the cold in winter. There was no case in which the eagerness, the surprise, the astonishment was not interesting if not pathetic. They were not expecting the Christmas holidays to offer them any suggestion of remembrance. It did not seem real that any one should stop and give them anything. Yet here was I, and apparently their wildest anticipations were outreached.

I cannot help thinking, as I close, of an old gray-haired Irish gentleman—for that he was, by every mark of refinement of feature and intelligence of eye—who had come so low as to be the perambulating representative of a restaurant, with a double sign strapped over his shoulders. His hair was thin, his face pale, his body obviously undernourished, but he carried himself with dignity and undisturbed resignation, though he must have been deeply conscious of his state. I saw him for a number of days during the winter season, walking up and down the west side of Sixth Avenue, and then I saw him no more. But during that time a sense of what it means to accept the slings and arrows of fortune with fortitude and equanimity burned itself deeply into my mind. He was so much better than that which he was compelled to do. He walked so patiently to and fro, his eyes sometimes closed, his lips repeating something. I wondered, what? Whether in the depths of this slough of his despond this man had not risen superior to his state, his mind on those high cold verities which after all are above the pointless little existence that we lead here, this existence with its petty

gauds and its pretty and petty vanities.   I hope so.
But I do know that a stinging sense of the slings and
arrows of fortune overcame me, never to be eradicated,
and I quoted to myself that arresting, forceful inquiry
of one William Shakespeare:

> "For who would bear the whip and scorns of time,
> The oppressor's wrong, the proud man's contumely,
> The pangs of despised love, the law's delay,
> The insolence of office, and the spurns
> That patient merit of the unworthy takes.
>   Who would fardels bear,
> To grunt and sweat under a weary life?"

Not, you, you think?   Boast not.   For after all, who
shall say what a day or a year or a lifetime may not
bring forth?   And with Whatley cannot we all say:
"There, but for the grace of God, go I"—a beggar, an
outcast of fortune, a sandwich man, no less, to whom the
meaning of life is that he shall be a foil to comfort, a
contrast to prosperity, a commentary on health.

To be the antithesis of what life would prefer to be
—what could be more degraded than that?

THE LOVE AFFAIRS OF LITTLE ITALY

ONE of the things that has always interested me about the several Italian sections of New York City is their love feuds. Every day and every hour, in all these sections, is being enacted those peculiarly temperamental and emotional things which we attribute more to dispositions that sensate rather than think. How often have I myself been an eye-witness to some climacteric conclusion, to some dreadful blood feud or opposition or contention—a swarthy Italian stabbing a lone woman in a dark street at night, a seemingly placid diner in some purely Italian restaurant rising to an amazing state of rage because of a look, a fancied insult, some old forgotten grudge, maybe, renewed by the sight of another. At one time, when I had personal charge of the Butterick publications, I was an immediate and personal witness to stabbings and shootings that took place under my very eye, some bleeding and fleeing adversary brushing me as he ran, to fall exhausted a little farther on. And mobs of Americans, not understanding these peculiarly deep-seated and emotional feuds, and resenting always the use of the knife or the stiletto, seeking to wreak summary vengeance upon those who, beyond peradventure, are in nowise governed by our theories or our conventions, but hark by other and more devious paths back into the Italy of the Middle Ages, and even beyond that.

The warmth of passion and tenderness that lies wrapped up in these wonderful southern quarters of our colder northern clime. The peculiarly romantic and marvelously involved series of dramatic episodes, feuds or fancies, loves or hates, politics or passion, such as would do honor to a mediæval love tale—the kind of episodes that have made the history of Italy as intricate as any in the world!

The section that has always interested me most is the one that lies between Ninety-sixth Street and One Hundred and Sixteenth on the East Side of Manhattan Island, and incloses all the territory that lies between Second Avenue and the East River. It is a wonderful section. Here, regardless of the presence of the modern tenement building and the New York policeman, you may see such a picture of Italian life and manners as only a visit to Naples and the vine-clad hills of southern Italy would otherwise afford.

Vigorous and often attractive maidens in orange and green skirts, with a wealth of black hair fluffed back from their foreheads, and yellow shawls and coral necklaces fastened about their necks; dark, somber-faced Italian men, a world of moods and passions sleeping in their shadowy eyes, decked out in bright Garibaldian shirts and soft slouch hats, their tight-fitting corduroy trousers drawn closely about their waists with a leather belt; quaint, cameo-like old men with earrings in their ears and hands like claws and faces seamed with the strongest and most sinister lines, and yet with eyes that flash with feeling or beam with tenderness; and old women, in all forms of color and clothing, who chatter and gesticulate and make the pavements resound with the excitement of their everyday bargaining.

This, truly, in so far as New York is concerned, is the region of the love feud and the balcony. If you will stand at any of the cross-streets that lead east from Second Avenue you will obtain a splendid panorama of the latter feature, window after window ornamented with a red or green or orange iron balcony and hung, in the summertime, with an array of green vines and bright flower-pots that invariably suggests the love scene of Shakespeare's famous play and the romantic love feeling of the south. Dark, poetic-looking Italians lean against doorjambs and open gateways and survey the surrounding neighborhood with an indolent and romantic eye. Plump Italian mothers gaze comfortably out of open windows, before which they sit and sew and watch their chubby little children romp and play in the streets. Fat, soft-voiced merchants, and active, graceful, song-singing Italian street venders ply their various vocations, the latter turning a wistful eye to every window, the former lolling contentedly in wooden chairs, the blessings of warmth and a little trade now and again being all that they require.

And from out these windows and within these doors hang or lounge those same maidens, over whom many a bloody feud has been waged and for whom (for a glance of the eyes or the shrug of the shoulder) many of these moody-faced, somber-eyed, love-brooding Romeos have whipped out their glistening steel and buried it in the heart of a hated rival. Girls have been stabbed here, been followed and shot (I have seen it myself); petty love-

conversations upon a street corner or in the adjacent
park between two ardent lovers have been interrupted by
the sudden appearance of a love frenzied Othello, who
could see nothing for it but to end the misery of his unre-
quited affection by plunging his knife into the heart of
his rival and into that of his fair but unresponsive sweetheart. They love and hate; and death is the solution
of their difficulties—death and the silence of the grave.

"She will not love me! Then she must die!"

The wonder of the colony is the frankness and freedom with which its members take to this solution. Actually, it would seem as if this to them were the only
or normal way out of a love tangle. And if you can
ever contrive an intelligent conversation with any of
them you will find it so. Lounge in their theaters, the
teatro marionette, their cafés, about the open doorways
and the street corners, and hear the frankness with which
they discuss the latest difficulty. Then you will see
for yourself how simple it all seems to them.

Vincenzo is enamored of his Elvina. So is Nicola.
They give each other black looks, and when Elvina is
seen by Vincenzo to walk openly with Nicola he broods
in silence, meditating his revenge.

One night, when the moon is high and the noisy thoroughfare is pulsating with that suppressed enthusiasm
which is a part of youth and passion and all the fervid
freshness of a warm July night, Vincenzo meets them
at the street corner. He is despondent, desperate. Out
comes his knife—click!—and the thing is done. On
the pavement lies Nicola bleeding. Elvina may be seen
running and screaming. She too is wounded, mayhap

to the death. Vincenzo runs and throws his hands dramatically over his head as he falls, mayhap shot or stabbed—by himself or another. Or Elvina kneels in the open street beside her lover and cries. Or Vincenzo, white-faced and calm, surrenders himself into the hands of the rough, loud swearing American policeman—and there you have it.

But ask of the natives, and see what it is they think. They will not have it that Vincenzo should not have done so, nor Elvina, nor Nicola. Love is love! Youth is youth! What would you? May not a man settle the affairs of his heart in his own way? *Perdi!*

And these crimes (as the law considers them), so common are they that it would be quite impossible to give more than a brief mention to any of a hundred or more that have occurred within as many as ten or fifteen years. Sometimes, as in the case of Tomasso Ceralli and Vincenzo Matti, it is a question of a married woman and an illegal passion. Sometimes, as in the case of Biegio Refino and Alessandro Scia, it is some poor cigarette-factory girl who, being used as a tool by one or more, has fallen into others' hands and so incensed all and brought into being a feud. Sometimes, as in the case of Mollinero and Pagnani, it is a bold, bad Carmen who is not sorry to see her lovers fight.

But these stories are truly legion and in some instances the police would never have been the wiser save for a man or a woman whom the neighbors could not get out of the way in time. Once caught, however, they come bustling into the nearest station house, these strange groups of wild, fantastic, disheveled men and women, and behind them, or before, the brawny officers of our colder clime, with their clubs and oaths and hoarse comments on the folly and the murderous indecency of it all—and all in an effort to inspire awe and a preventive fear that, somehow, can never be inspired. "These damned dagos, with their stilettos! These crazy wops!" But the melancholy Italian does not care for these commands or our laws. They are not for him. Let the cold, chilly American threaten; he will carry his stiletto anyhow. It is reserved as a last resource in the face of injustice or cruelty or the too great indifference of this world and of fate.

One of the most interesting of these love affairs that ever came to my personal attention was that of Vincenzo Cordi, street musician and, in a way, a ne'er-do-well, who became unduly enraged because Antonio Fellicitti, vegetable merchant, paid too marked attention to his sweetheart. These men, typical Italians of the quarter, knew each other, but there was no feeling until the affections of both were aroused by the charms of Maria Maresco, the pretty daughter of one of the laborers of the street.

According to the best information that could be obtained at the time, Cordi had been first in the affections of the girl, but Fellicitti arrived on the scene and won her away from him. Idling about the vicinity of her house in One Hundred and Fourteenth Street he had seen her and had fallen desperately in love.

Then there was trouble, for Cordi soon became aware of the defection which Fellicitti had caused, and told him so. "You keep away," was his threat. "Go, and come near her no more. If you do, I will kill you."

You can imagine the feeling which this conversation engendered. You can see the gallant Antonio, eyeing his jealous rival through the long, thin slits of his shadowy, southern eyes. He keep away? Ha! Ha! Vincenzo keep him away? Ha! Ha! If Maria but loved him, let Vincenzo rage. When the time came he would answer.

And of course the time came. It was of a Sunday evening in March, the first day on which the long cold winter broke and the sun came out and made the city summer-like. Thousands in this section filled the little park, with its array of green benches, to overflowing. Thousands more lounged in the streets and sunned themselves, or swarmed the cafés where was music and red wine and lights and conversation. Still other thousands sat by open windows or on the steps in front of open doors and gossiped with their neighbors—a true forerunner of the glorious summer to follow.

Then came the night, that glorious time of affection and good humor, when every Italian of this neighborhood is at his best. The moon was on high, a new moon, shining with all the thin delicacy of a pearl. Soft airs were blowing, clear voices singing; from every window streamed lamplight and laughter. It seemed as if all the beauty of spring had been crowded into a single hour.

On this occasion the fair Maria was lounging in front of her own doorstep when the lovesick Antonio came along. He was dressed in his best. A new red handkerchief was fastened about his neck, a soft crush hat set jauntily upon his forehead. Upon his hand was a ring, in the handkerchief a bright pin, and he was in his most cavalier mood. Together they talked, and as they observed the beauty of the night they decided to stroll to the little park a block away.

Somewhere in this thoroughfare, however, stood the jealous Vincenzo brooding. It was evident that he must have been concealed somewhere, watching, for when the two strolled toward the corner he was seen to appear and follow. At the corner, where the evening crowd was the thickest and the merriest—summer pleasure at its height, as it were—he suddenly confronted Antonio and drew his revolver.

"Ha!"

The astonished Antonio had no time to defend himself. He drew his knife, of course, but before he could act Vincenzo had fired a bullet into his breast and sent him reeling on his last journey.

Maria screamed. The crowd gathered. Friends of Antonio and Vincenzo drew knives and revolvers, and for a few moments it looked as if a feud were on. Then came the police, and with them the prosaic ambulance and patrol wagon—and another tragedy was recorded. Antonio was dead and Vincenzo severely cut and bruised.

And so it goes. They love desperately. They quarrel dramatically, and in the end they often fight and die, as we have seen. The brief, practical accounts of the newspapers give no least suggestion of the color, the emotion, the sorrow, the rage—in a way, the dramatic beauty—that attends them, nearly all.

CHRISTMAS IN THE TENEMENTS

THEY are infatuated with the rush and roar of a great metropolis. They are fascinated by the illusion of pleasure. Broadway, Fifth Avenue, the mansions, the lights, the beauty. A fever of living is in their blood. An unnatural hunger and thirst for excitement is burning them up. For this they labor. For this they endure a hard, unnatural existence. For this they crowd themselves in stifling, inhuman quarters, and for this they die.

The joys of the Christmas tide are no illusion with most of us, the strange exhibition of fancy, of which it is the name, no mockery of our dreams. Far over the wide land the waves of expectation and sympathetic appreciation constantly oscillate one with the other in the human breast, and in the closing season of the year are at last given definite expression. Rings and pins, the art of the jeweler and the skill of the dressmaker, pictures, books, ornaments and knickknacks— these with one great purpose are consecrated, and in the material lavishness of the season is seen the dreams of the world come true.

There is one region, however, where, in the terrific drag of the struggle for existence, the softer phases of this halcyon mood are at first glance obscure. It is a region of tall tenements and narrow streets where, crowded into an area of a few square miles, live and labor a million and a half of people. It is the old-time tenement area, leading almost unbrokenly north from Franklin Square to Fourteenth Street. Here, during these late December evenings, the holiday atmosphere is beginning to make itself felt. It is a region of narrow streets with tall five-story, even seven-story, tenements lining either side of the way and running thick as a river with a busy and toilsome throng.

The ways are already lined with carts of special Christmas goods, such as toys, candies, Christmas tree ornaments, feathers, ribbons, jewelry, purses, fruit, and in a few wagons small Christmas greens such as holly and hemlock wreaths, crosses of fir, balsam, tamarack pine and sprigs of mistletoe. Work has not stopped in the factories or stores, and yet these streets are literally packed with people, of all ages, sizes and nationalities, and the buying is lively. One man, who looks as though he might be a Bowery tough rather than a denizen of this particular neighborhood, is offering little three-, five- and ten-inch dolls which he announces as "genuine American beauties here. Three, five and ten." Another, a pale, full-bearded Jew, is selling little Christmas tree ornaments of paste or glass for a penny each, and in the glare of the newly-turned-on electric lights, it is not difficult to perceive that they are the broken or imperfect lots of the toy manufacturers who are having them hawked about during the eleventh hour before Christmas as the best way of getting rid of them. Other dusty, grim and raucous denizens are offering candy, mixed nuts, and other forms of special confections, at ten cents a pound, a price at which those who are used to the more expensive brands may instructively ponder.

Meats are selling in some of the cheaper butcher shops for ten, fifteen and twenty cents a pound, picked chickens in barrels at fifteen and twenty. A whole section of Elizabeth Street is given up to the sale of stale fish at ten and fifteen cents a pound, and the crowd of Italians, Jews and Bohemians who are taking advantage of these modest prices is swarming over the sidewalk and into the gutters. A four- or five-pound fish at fifteen cents a pound will make an excellent Christmas dinner for four, five or six. A thin, ice-packed and chemically-preserved chicken at fifteen or twenty cents a pound will do as much for another family. Onions, garlic, old cast-off preserves, pickles and condiments that the wholesale houses uptown have seen grow stale and musty on their shelves, can be had here for five, ten and fifteen cents a bottle, and although the combination is unwholesome it will be worked over as Christmas dinners for the morrow. Cheap, unsalable, stale, adulterated— these are the words that should be stamped on every bottle, basket and barrel that is here being scrambled over. And yet the purchasers would not be benefited any thereby. They must buy what they can afford. What they can afford is this.

The street, with its mass of life, lingers in this condition until six o'clock, when the great shops and factories turn loose their horde of workers. Then into the glare of these electric-lighted streets the army of shop girls and boys begins to pour. Here is a spectacle interesting and provocative of thought at all seasons, but trebly so on this particular evening. It is a shabby throng at best, commonplace in garb and physical appearance, but rich in the qualities of youth and enthusiasm, than which the world holds nothing more valuable.

Youth in all the glory of its illusions and its ambitions. Youth, in whom the cold insistence of life's physical limitations and the law have not as yet worked any permanent depression. Thousands are hurrying in every direction. The street cars which ply this area are packed as only the New York street car companies can pack their patrons, and that in cold, old, dirty and even vile cars. There are girls with black hair, and girls with brown. Some have even, white teeth, some shapely figures, some a touch of that persuasive charm which is indicated by the flash of an eye. There are poor dresses, poor taste, and poor manners mingled with good dresses, good taste and good manners. In the glow of the many lights and shadows of the evening they are hurrying away, with that lightness of spirit and movement which is the evidence of a long strain of labor suddenly relaxed.

"Do you think Santa Claus will have enough to fill that?" asks an officer, who is standing in the glare of a balsam- and pine-trimmed cigar store window, to a smartly dressed political heeler or detective who is looking on with him at the mass of shop-girls hurrying past. A shop-girl had gone by with her skirt cut to an inch or two below her knee, revealing a trim little calf and ankle.

"Eee yo! I hope so! Isn't she the candy?"

"Don't get fresh," comes quickly from the hurrying

figure as she disappears in the throng with a toss of her head. She has enjoyed the comment well enough, and the rebuke is more mischievous than angry.

"A goldfish! A goldfish! Only one cent!" cries a pushcart vendor, who is one of a thousand lining the pavements to-night, and at his behest another shop-girl, equally budding and youthful, stops to extract a penny from her small purse and carries away a thin, transparent prize of golden paste, for a younger brother, probably.

Others like her are being pushed and jostled the whole length of this crowded section. They are being nudged and admired as well as sought and schemed for. Whatever affections or attachments they have will be manifesting themselves to-night, as may be seen by the little expenditures they themselves are making. A goldfish of transparent paste or a half pound of candy, a cheap gold-plated stickpin, brooch or ring, or a handkerchief, collar or necktie bought of one of the many pushcart men, tell the story plainly enough. Sympathy, love, affection and passion are running their errant ways among this vast unspoken horde no less than among the more pretentious and well-remembered of the world.

And the homes to which they are hurrying, the places which are dignified by that title, but which here should have another name! Thousands upon thousands of them are turning into entry ways, the gloom or dirtiness or poverty of which should bar them from the steps of any human being. Up the dark stairways they are pouring into tier upon tier of human hives, in some instances not less than seven stories high and, of course, without an elevator, and by grimy landings they are sorted out and at last distributed each into his own cranny. Small, dark one-, two- and three-room apartments, where yet on this Christmas evening, one, and sometimes three, four and five are still at work sewing pants, making flowers, curling feathers, or doing any other of a hundred tenement tasks to help out the income supplied by the one or two who work out. Miserable one- and two-room spaces where ignorance and poverty and sickness, rather than greed or immorality, have made veritable pens out of what would ordinarily be bad enough. Many hundreds or thousands of others there are where thrift and shrewdness are making the best of very unfortunate conditions, and a hundred or two where actual abundance prevails. These are the homes. Let us enter.

Zorg is a Bohemian, and has a little two-room apartment. The windows of the only one which has windows looks into Elizabeth Street. It is a dingy apartment, unswept and unwhitewashed at present, where on this hearty Christmas Eve, himself, his wife, his wife's mother, and his little twelve-year-old son are laboring at a fair-sized deal table curling feathers. The latter is a simple task, once you understand it, dull, tedious, unprofitable. It consists in taking a feather in one hand, a knife in the other, and drawing the fronds quickly over the knife's edge. This gives them a very sprightly curl and can be administered, if the worker be an expert, by a single movement of the hand. It is paid for by the dozen, as such work is usually paid for in this region, and the ability to earn much more than sixty cents a day is not within the range of human possibility. Forty cents would be a much more probable average, and this is approximately the wages which these several individuals earn. Rent uses up three of the twelve dollars weekly income; food, dress, coal and light six more. Three dollars, when work is steady, is the sum laid aside for all other purposes and pleasures, and this sum, if no amusements were indulged in and no sickness or slackness of work befell, might annually grow to the tidy sum of one hundred and fifty-six dollars; but it has never done so. Illness invariably takes one part, lack of work a greater part still. In the long drag of weary labor the pleasure-loving instincts of man cannot be wholly restrained, and so it comes about that the present Christmas season finds the funds of the family treasury low.

It is in such a family as this that the merry Christmas time comes with a peculiar emphasis, and although the conditions may be discouraging, the efforts to meet it are almost always. commensurate with the means.

However, on this Christmas Eve it has been deemed a duty to have some diversion, and so, although the round of weary labor may not be thus easily relaxed, the wife has been deputed to do the Christmas shopping and has gone forth into the crowded East Side street, from which she has returned with a meat bone, a cut from a butcher's at twelve cents a pound, green pickles, three turnips, a carrot, a half-dozen small candles, and two or three toys, which, together with a small three-foot branch of hemlock, purchased earlier in the day, completes the

Christmas preparation for the morrow. Arba, the youngest, although like the others she will work until ten this Christmas Eve, is to have a pair of new shoes; Zicka, the next older, a belt for her dress. Mrs. Zorg, although she may not suspect, will receive a new market basket with a lid on it. Zorg—grim, silent, weary of soul and body—is to have a new fifteen-cent tie. There will be a tree, a small sprig of a tree, upon which will hang colored glass or paste balls of red and blue and green, with threads of popcorn and sprays of flitter-gold, all saved from the years before. In the light of early dawn to-morrow the youngest of the children will dance about these, and the richness of their beauty will be enjoyed as if they had not been so presented for the seventh and eighth time.

Thus it runs, mostly, throughout the entire region on this joyous occasion, a wealth of feeling and desire expressing itself through the thinnest and most meager material forms. About the shops and stores where the windows are filled with cheap displays of all that is considered luxury, are hosts of other children scarcely so satisfactorily supplied, peering earnestly into the world of make-believe and illusion, the wonder of it not yet eradicated from their unsophisticated hearts. Joy, joy—not a tithe of all that is represented by the expenditures of the wealthy, but only such as may be encompassed in a paper puff-ball or a tinsel fish, is here sought for and dreamed over, an earnest, child-heart-longing which may never again be gratified if not now. Horses, wagons, fire engines, dolls—these are what the thousands upon thousands of children whose faces are pressed closely against the commonplace window panes are dreaming about, and the longing that is thereby expressed is the strongest evidence of the indissoluble link which binds these weakest and most wretched elements of society to the best and most successful.

THE RIVERS OF THE NAMELESS DEAD

The body of a man was found yesterday in the North River at Twenty-fifth Street. A brass check, No. 21,600, of the New York Registry Company, was found on the body.—N. Y. Daily Paper.

THERE is an island surrounded by rivers, and about it the tide scurries fast and deep. It is a beautiful island, long, narrow, magnificently populated, and with such a wealth of life and interest as no island in the whole world before has ever possessed. Long lines of vessels of every description nose its banks. Enormous buildings and many splendid mansions line its streets.

It is filled with a vast population, millions coming and going, and is the scene of so much life and enthusiasm and ambition that its fame is, as the sound of a bell, heard afar.

And the interest which this island has for the world is that it is seemingly a place of opportunity and happiness. If you were to listen to the tales of its glory carried the land over and see the picture which it presents to the incoming eye, you would assume that it was all that it seemed. Glory for those who enter its walls seeking glory. Happiness for those who come seeking happiness. A world of comfort and satisfaction for all who take up their abode within it—an island of beauty and delight.

The sad part of it is, however, that the island and its beauty are, to a certain extent, a snare. Its seeming loveliness, which promises so much to the innocent eye, is not always easy of realization. Thousands come, it is true; thousands venture to reconnoiter its mysterious shores. From the villages and hamlets of the land is streaming a constant procession of pilgrims who feel that here is the place where their dreams are to be realized; here is the spot where they are to be at peace. That their hopes are not, in so many cases, to be realized, is the thing which gives a poignant tang to their coming. The beautiful island is not compact of happiness for all.

And the exceptional tragedy of it is that the waters which surround the beautiful island are forever giving evidence of the futility of the dreams of so many. If you were to stand upon any of its shores, where the tide scurries past in its never-ending hurry, or were to idle for a time upon its many docks and piers, which reach far out into the water and give lovely views of the sky and the gulls and the boats, you might see drifting past upon the bosom of the current some member of all the ambitious throng who, in time past, set his face toward the city, and who entered only to find that there was more of sorrow than of joy. Sad, white-faced maidens; grim, bearded, time-worn men; strange, strife-worn, grief-stricken women; and, saddest of all, children —soft, wan, tender children—floating in the waters which wash the shores of the island city.

And such waters! How green they look, how graceful, how mysterious! From far seas they come—strange,

errant, peculiar waters—prying along the shores of the
magnificent island; sucking and sipping at the rocks
which form its walls; whispering and gurgling about
the docks and piers, and flowing, flowing, flowing. Such
waters seem to be kind, and yet they are not so. They
seem to be cruel, and yet they are not so; merely indifferent these waters are—dark, strong, deep, indifferent.

And curiously the children of men who come to seek
the joys of the city realize the indifference and the
impartiality of the waters. When the vast and beautiful
island has been reconnoitered, when its palaces have
been viewed, its streets disentangled, its joys and its
difficulties discovered, then the waters, which are neither
for nor against, seem inviting. Here, when the great
struggle has been ended, when the years have slipped
by and the hopes of youth have not been realized; when
the dreams of fortune, the delights of tenderness, the
bliss of love and the hopes of peace have all been abandoned—the weary heart may come and find surcease.
Peace in the waters, rest in the depths and the silence
of the hurrying tide; surcease and an end in the chalice
of the waters which wash the shores of the beautiful
island.

And they do come, these defeated ones? Not one,
nor a dozen, nor a score every year, but hundreds and
hundreds. Scarcely a day passes but one, and sometimes
many, go down from the light and the show and the merriment of the island to the shores of the waters where
peace may be found. They stop on its banks; they reflect,
perhaps, on the joys which they somehow have missed;
they give a last, despairing glance at the wonderful scene

which once seemed so joyous and full of promise, and then yield themselves unresistingly to the unswerving strength of the powerful current and are borne away. Out past the docks and the piers of the wonderful city. Out past its streets, it palaces, its great institutions. Out past its lights, it colors, the sound of its merriment and its seeking, and then the sea has them and they are no more. They have accomplished their journey, the island its tragedy. They have come down to the rivers of the nameless dead. They have yielded themselves as a sacrifice to the variety of life. They have proved the uncharitableness of the island of beauty.

THE END